| M | E | N | S | A |
|---|---|---|---|---|
|   |   |   |   |   |
|   |   |   |   |   |
|   |   |   |   |   |
|   |   |   |   |   |

Using the letters M-E-N-S-A, complete the grid so that the same letter does not appear twice in any horizontal, vertical or corner-to-corner line.
*For solution see over.*

**Ken Russell** is a former London surveyor who lives in Kent. He is the Puzzle Editor of *Mensa*, a magazine issued free each month to Mensa's 20,000 UK members.

**Philip Carter** is a Yorkshire estimator and a Justice of the Peace. He is Puzzle Editor of the 'Mensa Puzzle Special Interest Group'.

## Solution

| M | E | N | S | A |
|---|---|---|---|---|
| S | A | M | E | N |
| E | N | S | A | M |
| A | M | E | N | S |
| N | S | A | M | E |

# The Mensa Puzzle Book

*Ken Russell
and Philip Carter*

WARNER BOOKS

A *Warner* Book

First published in Great Britain by Sphere Books Ltd 1988
Reprinted 1989, 1990, 1991 (twice)
Reprinted by Warner Books 1994
Reprinted 1995

Copyright © 1988 by Ken Russell and Philip Carter

ISBN 0 7515 1076 9

Printed in England by Clays Ltd, St Ives plc

Warner Books
A Division of
Little, Brown and Company (UK)
Brettenham House
Lancaster Place
London WC2E 7EN

# Authors' Note

This book is dedicated to our wives, both named Barbara, who have given us their support and encouragement in our endeavour to compile new and interesting puzzles, and have checked out the answers.

We also wish to acknowledge the assistance and advice given to us by Victor Serebriakoff, the International President of Mensa, who is a great puzzle innovator. We are indebted too to Harold Gale, the Mensa Chief Executive, a prolific puzzle composer, and we wish to thank the members of the British Mensa Committee who gave permission for use of the Mensa name in the title.

# What Is Mensa?

Mensa is a unique society. It is, basically, a social club – but a social club different from others. The only qualification for membership is a high score on an intelligence test. One person in fifty should qualify for membership; these people will come from all walks of life and have a wide variety of interests and occupations.

Mensa is the Latin word for table: we are a round-table society where no one has special precedence. We fill a void for many intelligent people otherwise cut off from contact with other good minds – contact that is important to them, but elusive in modern society. Besides being an origin of many new friendships, we provide members with a receptive but critical audience on which to try out new ideas.

Mensa is protean: its most visible feature is its diversity. It crosses the often artificial barriers which separate people from each other. It recruits, not like other societies by persuading people to think as they do, or by searching for a particular narrow common interest, but by scientifically selecting people who are able to think for themselves. Yet, although there appears little common ground and little surface agreement between members, we find there is an underlying unity which gives an unexpected strength to the society.

Mensa has three aims: social contact between intelligent people; research in psychology and the social sciences; and the identification and fostering of human intelligence. Mensa is an international society; it has more than 85,000 members. We have members of almost every occupation – business people, clerks, doctors, editors, factory workers, farm labourers, housewives, lawyers, police officers, politicians, soldiers, scientists, students, teachers – and of almost every age.

*Enquiries and applications to:*

Mensa
FREEPOST
Wolverhampton WV2 1BR

Mensa International
15 The Ivories
6–8 Northampton Street
London N1 2HV

# Puzzles

So that you don't inadvertently read the solution to the next puzzle while you are checking your answer, the solutions are in a different sequence from that of the puzzles.

# Nursery Rhyme Crossword

*Complete the crossword – the eight clues are contained in the narrative. Once you have solved the clues, place the answers in the correct positions.*

Little Miss Muffet sat on a tuffet having consumed light refreshment between breakfast and dinner, consisting of a liquid which was congealed and coagulated, and having taken a dose of laxative drug obtained from the bark of a tree.

Down came a diabolical, Hellish, Greek spider, which sat down beside her.

A document which had been altered and corrected made an ordinance or authoritative edict that the spider should travel back over its route.

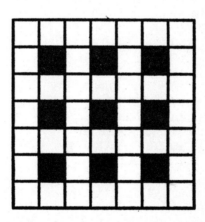

# Middle Words

Fill in the missing word which, when tacked on to the first word, forms a new word and, when placed in front of the second word, forms another word. For instance: EVER ..... HOUSE (5). Answer: GREEN.

1. BLUE .... BOY (4)
2. ARC ... RING (3)
3. BAR .... SAY (4)
4. RAG ... RAGE (3)
5. PAGE ... HEM (3)
6. OVER .... AGE (4)
7. TAR ... AWAY (3)
8. FOR ... TRESS (3)
9. LOT .. HER (2)
10. SEA ... NET (3)
11. CAN ... SURE (3)
12. NUT ... ELOPE (3)
13. NOW .... AFTER (4)
14. IMP ... OR (3)
15. BASE .... ON (4)
16. FLU .. DEAL (2)
17. DO ... NECK (3)
18. SO .... RATE (4)
19. PAD .... YARD (4)
20. IN .... AT (4)

# Needle

*Solution 49*

Parallel lines are drawn on the floor, each equidistant from the next. A needle is dropped at random. What are the odds that the needle will land touching or across one of the lines?

The needle's length is half of the distance between the lines.

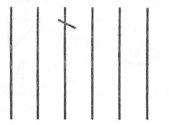

# Pair-words

*Solution 16*

Pair a word from list A with a word from list B, until you have ten matching pairs. There are two possible pairing words in list A with each word in list B and vice versa. There are two correct solutions.

| List A | List B |
|--------|--------|
| Dog | Toadstool |
| Perch | Halo |
| Umbrella | Passerine |
| Moon | Rain |
| Mandibles | Sirius |
| Shark | Planet |
| Thrush | Mackerel |
| Star | Fungus |
| Nimbus | Canine |
| Mushroom | Jaws |

Which of the figures, A or B, is logically the next in sequence?

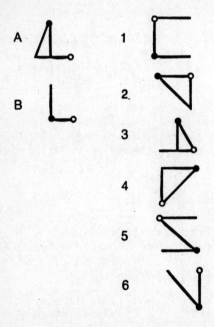

# Alphabet

Fill in the crossword using the twenty-six letters of the alphabet.

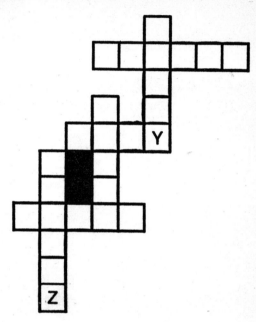

# Fruit

Supply the missing letters and find the fruit.

1. * V * C * D *
2. * R * N * E * R *
3. * E * C *
4. * U * K * E * E * R *
5. * E * O *
6. * A * P * E * R *
7. * R * N *
8. * O * A * B * R * Y
9. * A * T * L * U * E
10. * A * A * A
11. * A * D * R * N
12. * P * I * O *

# Collective Nouns

These twelve collective names have been mixed up. Rearrange them correctly.

Colony    of Birds
Horde     of Spiders
Den       of Wild Pigs
Clutter   of Crows
Nest      of Snakes
Park      of Elks
Doylt     of Ferrets
Gang      of Machine Guns
Business  of Swine
Volery    of Artillery
Hover     of Gnats
Drift     of Frogs

# Routes

How many different routes are there from A to B always travelling South or East?
There is a simple rule.

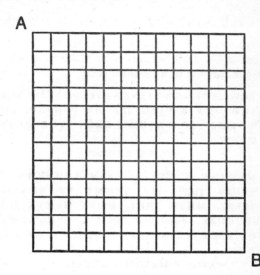

# Dictionary Solution 140

Find a word used commonly in the English language which has five consecutive vowels embedded in it.

## Three Cryptograms Solution 71

Each Cryptogram is a straight substitution code, where one letter of the alphabet has been replaced by another. Each of the three is in a different code.

1. E TVPCWFWPTW XB E IENRWFXPI VC XZJVFNEPN
   JWVJHW ARV BXPIHU TEP MV PVNRXPI LON
   NVIWNRWF TEP MWTXMW NREN PVNRXPI TEP
   LW MVPW.

   — CFWM EHHWP

2. AZFWVUKF XIWFF ... VBH KQWFWVO VZ
   PZEHVHFF JBKV WX TZWMT VZ BKAAHM
   VZRZEEZJ, MHYV JHHI, MHYV RZMVB KMG
   MHYV OHKE. KMG VZ BKCH VBH KQWFWVO
   KPVHEJKEGX VZ HYAFKWM JBO WV GWGM'V
   BKAAHM.

   — XWE JWMXVZM UBLEUBWFF.

3. G KPFIFPR JK G DIYC PIQ QKU DAUF PIQ HGF'Z
   KVUBB ZAU DIYC PIQ SJYKZ ZAIQXAZ IS.

   — MQYZ MGHAGYGHA.

## Addenda Solution 124

How many words can you think of whose only consonants are D and N? You should find thirty-five or more! (Y counts as a vowel, hyphens allowed.)

Here are thirty-two three-letter sections, which make up sixteen six-letter words. Find the words.

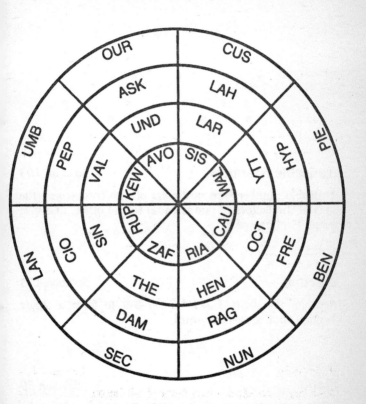

## Spots

*Solution 41*

Move three spots to turn the triangle upside down.

## Amicable Numbers

*Solution 103*

Amicable numbers are rare pairs of numbers, where the sum of the factors of one is equal to the other, and vice versa. Find one pair.

## Fraction

*Solution 133*

Arrange the digits 1-2-3-4-5-6-7-8-9 to form a single fraction that equals one-third.

## Piano

*Solution 50*

What is the longest word which can be played on the piano? That is, a word which can be made up using only the letters A-B-C-D-E-F-G as many times as possible.

# Fieldwork

*Solution 60*

This field, which measures 112 m × 75 m, can be split up into thirteen square plots, with all dimensions whole metres. Fill in the dimensions.

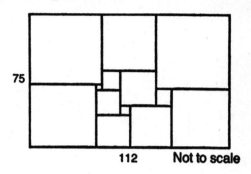

75

112    Not to scale

# No Hyphens

*Solution 83*

Can you think of five words – of four, five, six, seven and eight letters – each of which contains a different set of three alphabetically consecutive letters?

# Triangles

Solution 96

How many triangles in this figure?

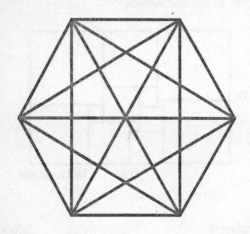

# Odd One

Solution 28

Which is the odd one out?

AS
BE
IN
NET
OF
TO
UP
WE
NEEDLES

# Nursery Rhyme Crossword

*Hidden in the narrative are eight clues. Find them, solve them, and place the answers in the correct positions in the grid.*

Pussy cat, pussy cat, from the Middle East, with long silky hair and a thick tail, where have you been? I've been to the very middle part of London to see the Queen and her royal sons, who accuse by legal processes, sets of co-ordinated doctrines. Pussy cat, pussy cat, what did you there? I frightened some animals with strong incisors with a bend inwards, one of which lies snugly embedded under a chair.

# Killer

*Solution 30*

Arthur, Bill and Charlie were questioned about the murder of Donald. Evidence at the scene of the crime indicated that a left-handed man was the murderer. Each suspect, one of whom was the murderer, made two statements as follows:

**Arthur**
1. I am not left-handed
2. I did not kill Donald

**Bill**
1. I am left-handed
2. I did not kill Donald

**Charlie˙**
1. I am not left-handed
2. A left-handed man killed Donald.

The police discovered that only two statements are true. Only one of the three suspects was not left-handed.

Who killed Donald?


# Palindrome

*Solution 147*

Find an eleven-letter palindrome which is a word in the dictionary.

# Scrabble

Using the following letters, making five five-letter words, score 200 or more.

| | Score | | Score |
|---|---|---|---|
| A | 1 | M | 3 |
| A | 1 | M | 3 |
| E | 1 | O | 1 |
| E | 1 | O | 1 |
| E | 1 | P | 3 |
| G | 2 | Q | 10 |
| H | 4 | R | 1 |
| I | 1 | T | 1 |
| I | 1 | U | 1 |
| J | 8 | X | 8 |
| K | 5 | Y | 4 |
| L | 1 | Y | 4 |
| | | Z | 10 |

# Crossword

Select the correct letter from the three which correspond to each number and complete the crossword.

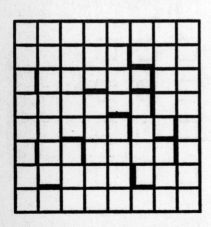

| | |
|---|---|
| 7 | 3 | 2 | 2 | 1 | 1 | 6 | 7 |
| 1 | 2 | 1 | 3 | 2 | 7 | 2 | 2 |
| 7 | 3 | 8 | 5 | 6 | 9 | 1 | 2 |
| 7 | 5 | 3 | 4 | 2 | 2 | 7 | 6 |
| 7 | 7 | 7 | 2 | 6 | 3 | 7 | 1 |
| 5 | 3 | 7 | 8 | 1 | 5 | 7 | 3 |
| 1 | 1 | 3 | 2 | 7 | 7 | 3 | 2 |
| 7 | 4 | 2 | 2 | 6 | 2 | 6 | 7 |

| 1 | A B C |
|---|---|
| 2 | D E F |
| 3 | G H I |
| 4 | J K L |
| 5 | M N O |
| 6 | P Q R |
| 7 | S T U |
| 8 | V W X |
| 9 | Y Z |

18

# D-I-Y Crossword

You have to fill in the two crosswords. Unfortunately all
the answers are mixed up.

| | | |
|---|---|---|
| CLUSTERS | LED | OPERATIC |
| BY | TOO | TROT |
| DISABLES | EPICENE | VASSAL |
| DEDUCES | EAT | TAW |
| SPATTERS | ODD | BETTERED |
| NEE | REAM | TOE |
| SCUDDED | APE | WE |
| SON | INLET | SWADDLES |
| AIDE | STUDIO | LEERS |
| ENTREE | LINDEN | EEL |
| BOARDERS | ERE | RACE |
| RESET | DECLARED | BROW |
| ARSON | TINES | DEEPS |
| BEDEVILS | DECLARES | SYSTEMS |
| CUSSED | COD | OR |
| LANE | SLEET | |

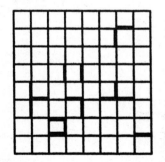
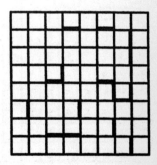

# Number Crossword

In the first grid answers start from a number and finish on the next highest number and so on.

To find the answers convert the numbers in the second grid to the selection of letters in the key, choosing the correct one each time.

| | | | | | | | | |
|---|---|---|---|---|---|---|---|---|
| 1 | 5 | | | | | | | 4 |
| 10 | | | 13 | | | 12 | | 7 |
| | | | | | | | | |
| | 17 | | | | | | 15 | |
| | | | | | | | | |
| | | | | | | | 14 | |
| | | | | 16 | | | | |
| 11 | | 8 | | | | 9 | | 6 |
| 3 | | | | | | | | 2 |

| 1 | A B C |
|---|---|
| 2 | D E F |
| 3 | G H I |
| 4 | J K L |
| 5 | M N O |
| 6 | P Q R |
| 7 | S T U |
| 8 | V W X |
| 9 | Y Z |

| | | | | | | | | |
|---|---|---|---|---|---|---|---|---|
| 6 | 2 | 7 | 3 | 5 | 1 | 5 | 9 | 2 |
| 1 | 2 | 5 | 1 | 3 | 6 | 2 | 5 | 2 |
| 3 | 3 | 2 | 7 | 5 | 7 | 2 | 3 | 2 |
| 5 | 2 | 3 | 5 | 5 | 5 | 1 | 1 | 2 |
| 6 | 1 | 1 | 6 | 5 | 5 | 2 | 1 | 6 |
| 6 | 1 | 7 | 5 | 5 | 2 | 1 | 7 | 1 |
| 2 | 3 | 1 | 5 | 7 | 6 | 7 | 2 | 8 |
| 2 | 2 | 2 | 2 | 1 | 3 | 7 | 2 | 2 |
| 6 | 5 | 7 | 1 | 2 | 4 | 2 | 2 | 6 |

# Africa

*Solution 73*

Moving in any direction, including diagonally, find ten African countries in the grid. No square is used more than once in any word.

# Number

*Solution 88*

Which three-digit number has the most factors?

# Synonyme

*Solution 156*

Find a French word and an English word which are synonyms and are only made up of vowels (Y counts as a vowel).

# Integers

In which of these five groups are there two numbers, one of them the square of an integer and the other the cube of a different integer?

|      |     |     |     |     |     |
|------|-----|-----|-----|-----|-----|
| (A)  | 4   | 6   | 8   | 10  | 12  |
| (B)  | 6   | 9   | 12  | 15  | 36  |
| (C)  | 8   | 15  | 27  | 32  | 64  |
| (D)  | 36  | 42  | 49  | 57  | 81  |
| (E)  | 27  | 96  | 125 | 189 | 216 |

# Eight-pointed Star

Distribute the numbers 1 to 16 around the nodes, so that each of the eight lines adds up to the same number.

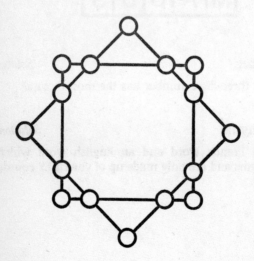

22

# Nursery Rhyme Crossword

*Hidden in the narrative are eight clues. You have to find them, solve them, and place the answers in the correct positions in the grid.*

As an enormous gigantic man, who lived in a town in India of which the letter occurring at the beginning was B, was smoking one very hot day, whilst the clock was making melodious, harmonious, attuned sounds, a bird who was a large pouched water fowl appeared suddenly and flew away with his pipe through a fence which was a structure of cross-laths with interstices serving as a screen, with the absolute positive assurance that it would return, which grieved, angered and irritated the fat man of B.

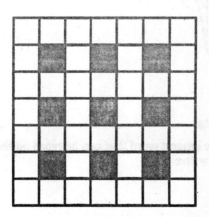

# Triangles
*Solution 101*

How many triangles in this figure?

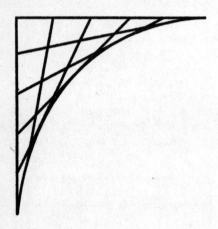

# Typewriter
*Solution 2*

What is the longest word that can be typed on the top row of the typewriter?

# Pyramid

*Solution 112*

Concealed in the pyramid is a fifteen-letter word. You may only visit each room once but may pass along the peripheral passage as much as you like. What is the word?

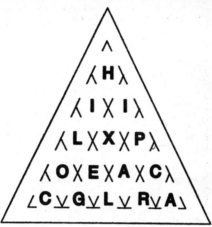

# Fibonacci

*Solution 141*

In a triangle where the length of each side is a different Fibonacci number, this formula gives the area of the triangle – or does it?

$$(2A \times \frac{C}{B}) + (2B \times \frac{C}{A}) + (2C \times \frac{B}{A})$$

# E-frame

Each horizontal and vertical line includes the consonants of a word which can be completed only by adding the vowel 'E'. The two-digit number at the end of each line indicates the number of consonants and 'E' vowels. For instance, 42 stands for 4 consonants and 2 vowels.

Each letter in the grid is used once only, and all the letters must be used.

**Clues**

| Across | Down |
|--------|------|
| 1 Headgear | 1 Birds |
| 2 Three-masted vessel | 2 Postpone |
| 3 Old person | 3 Makes mistakes |
| 4 Restore | 4 Fasten |
| 5 Give out | 5 Scolding woman |
| 6 Staggered | 6 Avoid |
| 7 Plan | 7 Whirlpool |

|   | 1 | 2 | 3 | 4 | 5 | 6 | 7 |    |
|---|---|---|---|---|---|---|---|----|
| 1 | W | S | T | R | R | B | Y | 42 |
| 2 | Z | D | R | C | C | C | B | 32 |
| 3 | S | G | Z | S | H | R | D | 33 |
| 4 | R | R | S | W | W | H | N | 32 |
| 5 | R | F | R | W | P | W | T | 32 |
| 6 | T | R | R | R | T | S | D | 44 |
| 7 | N | C | M | H | S | S | D | 42 |
|   | 41 | 32 | 31 | 41 | 41 | 42 | 31 |   |

# Word Search

Answers can be found in the crossword reading in any direction. Every letter is used, some letters more than once.

1. Slender spear
2. Iron tripod
3. Silky-coated dog
4. Afternoon nap
5. Sets of lines diverging from a point
6. Foolish person
7. Ways of looking
8. Ventures
9. Of kings
10. Drink
11. Recipient
12. Reasoned contentiously
13. Above average height
14. Talker
15. Writing fluid
16. Suit
17. Noticed
18. Money
19. Snake
20. Wrecked buildings
21. Garland of flowers
22. Otherwise

| R | S | I | E | S | T | A |
|---|---|---|---|---|---|---|
| S | E | N | E | E | S | S |
| L | N | K | V | S | A | P |
| L | A | I | A | L | A | E |
| A | R | G | U | E | D | C |
| T | A | K | E | R | P | T |
| I | I | D | A | R | E | S |

# Square

Divide the square into four identical sections. Each section must contain the same nine letters, which can be arranged into a familiar nine-letter word.

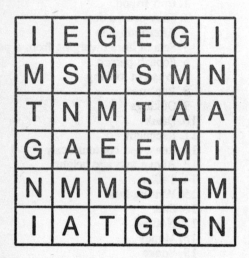

# Vowel

Each letter of the alphabet when sounded can be rhymed with a word or words, except for one. (For example: W = trouble you.)

Which is the exception?

## Pair-words

*Solution 102*

| List A | List B |
|--------|--------|
| Eagle | Range |
| Stirrup | Foot |
| Metacarpus | Griffin |
| Firing | Hand |
| Iris | Pin |
| Metatarsus | Eyrie |
| Maiden | Bone |
| Hippogriff | Eye |
| Mountain | Girl |
| Needle | Horse |

Pair a word from list A with a word from list B until you have ten matched pairs. Each word in list A has two possible pair-words in list B. Each word in list B has two possible pair-words in list A. There are two correct solutions.

## Highest Number

*Solution 67*

What is the highest number that can be obtained from the digits 1111, arranging them in any way and using any standard mathematical symbols?

Identify one word in the grid which meets all four conditions.

A. It is in an across line which contains two words connected with *horse*.
B. It is in a down line which contains two words connected with *weight*.
C. It does not appear in a line across or down which contains a word connected with *tea*.
D. It has no connection itself with *horse*, *weight* or *tea*.

| CLAY | PENNY | POOR | CHINA | PARTY |
|------|-------|------|-------|-------|
| SHOE | TURN | HEAVY | CHEESE | HOBBY |
| QUAR-TER | CHEST-NUT | GRAIN | FLESH | POUND |
| WORK | FLAG | COPY | POWER | UNCLE |
| SOCK | STONE | DANCE | CART | LIGHT |

# Clueless Crossword

In each square are four letters. Your task is to cross out three of each four, leaving one letter in each square, so the crossword is made up in the usual way with interlocking words.

| E T / P A | T R / N O | Q H / O P | C U / L F | T V / E I | I T / M R | Y E / A N |
|---|---|---|---|---|---|---|
| R N / H E | | | R A / O U | | | X Y / O N |
| T L / K E | R O / A E | T E / N F | O G / N P | I R / A E | O N / R S | N T / W O |
| O N / A T | | G U / I E | | I N / G R | | I P / A E |
| I N / S G | O U / R T | N S / O N | A P / H L | D G / I O | E A / N L | N G / L D |
| Y S / I R | | | E S / O N | | | N C / E U |
| C Y / H M | A I / M E | N E / R A | T N / D H | W L / P O | W R / E A | Y R / S T |

# Letter Search

Consider the grid. Now answer these questions –

1. What letter comes just above the letter just after the letter just below the letter just below the letter 'I'?

2. What letter comes midway between the letters which come midway between the letters 'W' and 'C' and the letters 'N' and 'H'?

3. What letter comes just after the letter just below the letter just below the letter just after the letter midway between the letters just after the letters 'I' and 'X'?

4. What letter comes just before the letter just below the letter just before the letter just below the letter just below the letter just after the letter which comes midway between the letters just after the letter 'M' and just before the letter 'A'?

| I | Q | G | M | D |
|---|---|---|---|---|
| H | B | V | Y | T |
| X | R | K | A | O |
| N | E | U | L | F |
| W | S | P | J | C |

# Missing Letters

*Solution 106*

What letters should the empty sections contain?

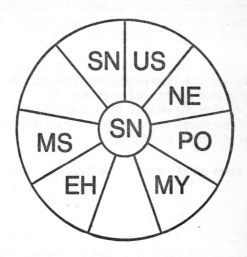

# Eleven

*Solution 77*

Seven different playing cards from ace to seven are shaken in a hat, then taken out singly and placed in a row.

Under what conditions would the seven-digit number formed by the row be divisible by eleven?

# Head to Head

*Solution 138*

Four white ants travelling in one direction meet four black ants travelling in the opposite direction on a narrow path. There is no room to pass on either side and they stop facing each other. The four ants in each group are nose to tail and there is the length of one ant between the two groups.

Each ant can only travel forwards but is able to jump over one ant at a time (again only forwards). No ant is allowed to land on the back of another ant.

How do they all pass each other, using the two possible forward movements only, and continue on their journey?

Try it with eight matchsticks.

1    2    3    4        5    6    7    8

# Cheque

*Solution 134*

A woman cashed a cheque at her bank. The teller misread the pounds as pence and the pence as pounds. The woman put away the correct amount of the cheque and with the dishonest profit purchased an article for £1.52. The amount she had remaining was half the original cheque's value. What was the cheque's value?

## Collective Nouns

*Solution 69*

These twelve collective names have been mixed up. Rearrange them correctly.

| | |
|---|---|
| Siege | of Hermits |
| Trip | of Harpers |
| Husk | of Larks |
| Exaltation | of Cranes |
| Melody | of Nightingales |
| Observance | of Owls |
| Watch | of Rabbits |
| Tribe | of Sheep |
| Kennel | of Hares |
| Parliament | of Goats |
| Colony | of Hounds |
| Cry | of Raches |

## Candles

*Solution 34*

One candle is guaranteed to burn for six hours, the other for four hours. They are both lit at the same time. After some time one is twice as long as the other. For how long have they been burning?

## Gloves

*Solution 113*

In a darkened room there is a box of mixed gloves, twenty-five pairs of black, twenty-three pairs of red, and twenty-one pairs of white. How many gloves must you take out without seeing them to be certain of taking out a matched pair (left and right of the same colour)?

*Hidden in the narrative are eight clues. Find them, solve them, and place the answers in the correct positions in the grid.*

There was an erratic, circuitous, man, who was an unsociable isolationist, who walked a crooked mile, and found a sixpence which was not of regular and even appearance, against a crooked stile, the vertical members of which incorporated an ingenious method of curvature in order to appear parallel.

He bought a crooked cat, removed the application of pressure and stress caused by its crooked collar, and it then caught a crooked mouse, and they all took up tenancy in a little crooked domicile on wheels, which was motivated by crooked machines which converted mechanical energy into electrical energy.

# Carriages

Solution 159

Supply the missing letters

1. * A * O * S * L *
2. * A * D * U
3. * R * S * K *
4. * R * U * H * M
5. * E * L * N
6. * A * O * C * E
7. * U * R * Y
8. * A * R * O * E
9. * U * G *
10. * H * N * R * D * N

# Antigrams

Solution 39

Antigrams are anagrams in which the letters of a word are reorganized to form a word or phrase meaning the opposite. In each case the answer is one word.

1. I limit arms
2. Is it legal? No
3. Fine tonic
4. Nice to imports
5. Aim to condemn
6. Tear no veils
7. Archsaints
8. Are advisers
9. More tiny
10. Care is noted

# Nines

When the sum of the digits of a number will divide exactly by nine, then the number itself will also divide by nine – for example, 2673: 2 + 6 + 7 + 3 = 18. With this in mind, place the digits into the grid so that each horizontal and vertical line, when read both forwards and backwards, will divide exactly by nine.

1,1,1
2,2,2
3,3,3,3
4,4,4,4
5,5
6,6
7
8,8,8
9,9,9

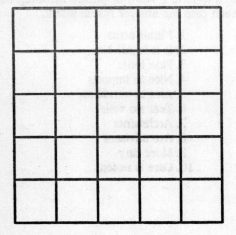

# Fish

*Solution 44*

Start at the centre square and track from square to square horizontally, vertically and diagonally to find eight kinds of fish. Every letter is used once only. Finish at the top right-hand square.

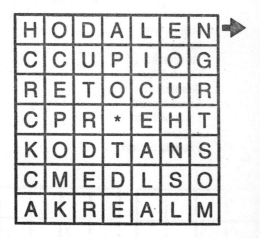

# Ferry

*Solution 72*

I have to ferry three animals across the river, a tiger, a hippo, and a lamb. The boat will only take two, myself and one animal. I cannot leave the tiger and hippo together because they will fight, I cannot leave the tiger and lamb together, but I can leave the hippo and lamb. How do I get them across?

# Magic Squares

Answers to the clues are all five-letter words. When the answers are placed in the correct position in the correct grid, two magic squares will be formed, so that the same five words can be read both across and down.

**Clues (in no particular order/grid)**
Slow
Lukewarm
Bring out
Haystacks
Greek letter
Scholar
Lowest point
Lock of hair
Escape
Foolish person

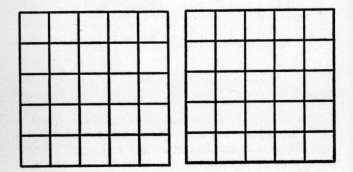

## Not Another *pi* Puzzle!

*Solution 119*

This is definitely not another *pi* puzzle, and any similarity is purely coincidental.

Starting at the arrow, find a way by which, if you insert all the four arithmetical signs (multiplication, division, addition, subtraction), two of them twice, in the blank squares and carry out all the operations in sequence, you obtain the answer 6 as shown.

| 1 |   | 4 |   | 1 |
|---|---|---|---|---|
|   | 2 | = | 6 |   |
| 3 |   | 9 |   | 5 |

↑

## Sequence

*Solution 6*

What is the next number in this sequence?

17, 23, 5, 18, 20, 25, –

## Middle Word
*Solution 108*

Fill in the missing four-letter word which, when tacked on to the first word, forms a new word, and when placed in front of the second word forms another word.

1. FORE .... AWAY
2. JAIL .... CAGE
3. MAIN .... FALL
4. PUFF .... COCK
5. SLAP .... BOOT
6. ROSE .... PULP
7. BUSY .... WORK
8. DOWN .... RATE
9. PEAR .... STAY
10. JUMP .... CASE

## Odd One Out
*Solution 135*

Which of these figures is the odd one out?

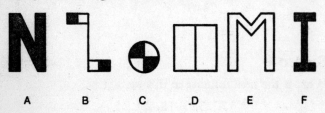

A     B     C     D     E     F

# Dances

Work from square to square vertically, horizontally or diagonally to find nineteen kinds of dance. Letters can be used more than once, but not in the same word. All letters in the grid are used.

| K | R | U | M | B | U | J | I |
|---|---|---|---|---|---|---|---|
| A | U | G | E | A | L | Q | G |
| M | Z | N | O | R | N | L | S |
| T | A | H | L | F | P | E | E |
| L | W | I | K | O | I | R | T |
| T | I | A | S | P | A | V | T |
| U | C | K | E | T | G | V | O |
| Q | M | I | N | U | E | J | I |

# Pair-words
*Solution 8*

| List A | List B |
|--------|--------|
| Canasta | Orange |
| Joan | Arc |
| Thrush | Canaster |
| Kibitzer | Leaf |
| Green | Lark |
| Segment | Spectator |
| Tobacco | Bird |
| Watcher | Azure |
| Sky | Rose |
| Bud | Cards |

Pair a word from list A with a word from list B until you have ten matched pairs. Each word in list A has two possible pair-words in list B. Each word in list B has two possible pair-words in list A. There are two correct solutions.

# Grandsons Galore
*Solution 136*

Grandpa Gubbins, whose age was somewhere between fifty and seventy, was fond of telling his friends: 'Each of my sons has as many sons as brothers, and the combined number of my sons and grandsons is precisely the same as the number of my years.'

How old was Gubbins?

# Steps

Solution 126

Commence with a word on the top line, then move sideways, down or diagonally, tacking the next word on the end to form a two-part compound word.

Carry on, and use sixteen words to form fifteen compound words. After your first move you can also go upwards.

*Example:*

WHIM–PER
    PER–SON

| WHIM | BREAK | SUP | PENNY | CURRANT |
|------|-------|------|-------|---------|
| FAST | PER | PIECE | BUN | WEIGHT |
| NET | SON | TIME | MEAL | BATH |
| HER | STEP | TABLE | COCK | PIT |
| FATHER | RING | VALVE | BALL | BOY |
| LET | WORM | SCREW | CAP | SIZE |

# Can You Help?

Solution 59

My friend Ali sells carpets. When he has to measure the area of a carpet, he squares up the average of the two sides.

I told him his answer would always be too large.

What else should he do to make his system accurate?

# Letters

Solution 97

In the diagram are six sections containing letters of the alphabet. In each section one letter is missing. What is the missing letter in each section and why?

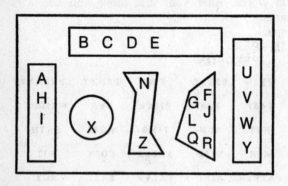

# Work It Out

Solution 12

Study the numbers in each circle and work out the number which, logically, is missing from the third circle.

# Nursery Rhyme Crossword

*Hidden in the narrative are eight clues. Find them, solve them, and place the answers in the correct positions in the grid.*

I had a little nut tree, nothing would it bear, but silver nutmegs and orange- and lemon-coloured finger-shaped fruits. The King (who relinquishes his throne shortly, and releases from jail all prisoners) of Spain's daughter, whose stylish hair was knotted at the back of her head, together with females of the same family, came to visit me, travelling by an air travel company, all for the sake of my little nut tree, which grows close by the root of a Chinese and Tibetan plant.

## Bridges

*Solution 155*

Two islands in a river are connected to each other and the shore by seven bridges. Starting anywhere, is it possible to cross each of the seven bridges without crossing any of them twice?

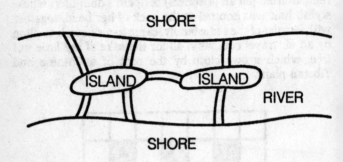

## Sixes

*Solution 25*

Can you find two words which contain six consecutive consonants?

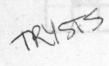

# Alphabet
*Solution 104*

Use the twenty-six letters of the alphabet to complete the nine words.

ABCDEFGHIJKLM
NOPQRSTUVWXYZ

1. * A * L O *
2. * * P L *
3. * A * S
4. * O * * *
5. * * Z *
6. A * O *
7. * U * * E
8. * E * E *
9. * O * *

# Children
*Solution 17*

A woman has nine children, born at regular intervals. The sum of the square of their ages is equal to the square of her own.

What are the ages of the children?

# Pronouns
*Solution 68*

*Chewed* contains two complete pronouns – he and we.

Find a six-letter word that contains five complete pronouns.

YOU
US
HE
WE
SHEWES

# Run Around

Two discs, exactly the same size, and, therefore, the same circumference, touch each other as shown. The bottom disc remains stationary while the top disc revolves round it once completely, always remaining touching. After the top disc has made its one complete circuit round the bottom disc, how many times has it rotated through 360 degrees?

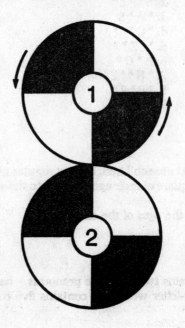

# Pyramid

*Solution 146*

Using only the letters D,E,I,M,P,R and T, fill in the pyramid so that each horizontal line forms a word, and each word consists of the same letters as the word above it (in any order), plus one additional letter. You must use all seven letters. (Nine-letter word base.)

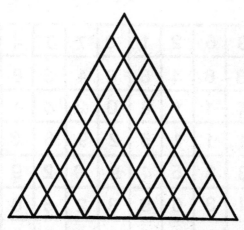

# Reverse

*Solution 153*

Find an eight-letter word, with or without a hyphen, which has all its letters in reverse alphabetical order. (Double letters are permitted).

*Example:* **Troll.**

# Square Numbers

Each horizontal and vertical line contains the digits of a four-figure square number. The digits are always in the right order, but not necessarily adjacent. Each digit is used once only, and they are all used. Find the sixteen four-figure numbers.

| 3 | 5 | 2 | 1 | 8 | 7 | 3 | 4 |
|---|---|---|---|---|---|---|---|
| 8 | 8 | 4 | 8 | 6 | 4 | 3 | 8 |
| 4 | 1 | 1 | 6 | 0 | 2 | 4 | 1 |
| 1 | 1 | 1 | 5 | 2 | 9 | 6 | 6 |
| 8 | 8 | 5 | 4 | 9 | 9 | 2 | 9 |
| 1 | 3 | 6 | 9 | 3 | 2 | 6 | 0 |
| 9 | 6 | 6 | 9 | 1 | 0 | 4 | 4 |
| 1 | 2 | 3 | 0 | 6 | 1 | 4 | 0 |

# Squares

*Solution 150*

Eight square pieces of paper, all exactly the same size, have been placed on top of each other, overlapping as shown. List the eight squares of paper in the correct order, from the top sheet down to the bottom sheet.

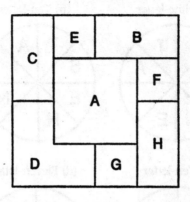

# Catch a Fish

*Solution 20*

Can you guess these fish?

1. One and Only
2. Rest precariously
3. Act clumsily
4. Low-pitched voice
5. Pointed weapon
6. Complain

# Overlapping Words

Read clockwise to find the word in each circle. The number of letters in each word is indicated. You supply the missing letters.

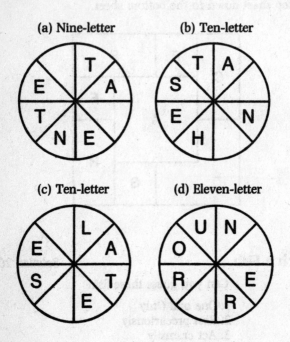

(a) Nine-letter

(b) Ten-letter

(c) Ten-letter

(d) Eleven-letter

# Squares

*Solution 24*

Can the three squares be drawn without taking the pen off the paper, intersecting any line or going over any part of a line twice?

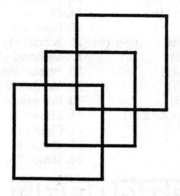

# Odd and Even

*Solution 105*

Find an eleven-letter word whose odd letters spell out a word, and whose even letters also spell out a word.

# Word Search

Answers will be found in straight lines in the grid in any direction. Letters are sometimes used more than once.

1. Insolent pride (6)
2. Of fish scale (6)
3. Water spirit (6)
4. Zinc (7)
5. Mythical sea monster (6)
6. Fortress (4)
7. Gold coin (5)
8. Fine silk (5)
9. Encircle (5)
10. Hunting ground (5)
11. Evidence (5)

12. Nut (5)
13. Beverage (3)
14. Part of tree (4)
15. Lease (4)
16. Female (4)
17. Gathered (4)
18. Female sheep (3)
19. Merriment (3)
20. Receptacle (3)
21. Know (3)
22. Chest (3)
23. Maim (4)
24. Metal (3)

# I-Frame

Each horizontal and vertical line includes the consonants of a word which can be completed by adding only a number of 'I' vowels.

The two-figure number at the end of each line indicates the number of consonants and vowels. For instance, 63 indicates 6 consonants and 3 'I' vowels.

Each letter in the grid is used only once, and all letters must be used.

**Across**
1. Stork-like bird
2. Boisterous sport
3. Very coldly
4. Lighting
5. Lazily
6. Unlawful
7. Drinking
8. Making impact

**Down**
1. Move stealthfully
2. Impression
3. Plant
4. Dwell long on point
5. Bodies of warriors
6. Batting turn
7. Boundlessness
8. Public houses

|   | 1 | 2 | 3 | 4 | 5 | 6 | 7 | 8 |    |
|---|---|---|---|---|---|---|---|---|----|
| 1 | G | T | B | S | S | S | N | S | 22 |
| 2 | K | S | R | N | N | N | J | N | 41 |
| 3 | N | N | L | C | M | N | F | Y | 32 |
| 4 | N | G | T | T | N | N | Y | G | 53 |
| 5 | D | M | S | Y | P | N | N | L | 31 |
| 6 | L | T | C | S | S | G | T | L | 43 |
| 7 | C | R | G | M | N | B | B | N | 53 |
| 8 | H | P | M | P | G | N | N | G | 63 |
|   | 52 | 52 | 22 | 42 | 32 | 52 | 53 | 31 |   |

# Nursery Rhyme Crossword

*Solution 62*

*The clues to the crossword are hidden in the narrative. Find the clues, solve them and place the answers in the grid.*

The man in the moon, who was one of the searchers for truth, came down too soon from one of the bodies revolving round the sun. He landed on a large treeless tract of grassland, on a surface covered in ridges and furrows. He had consumed too much and burnt his mouth whilst supping cold plum pudding. He had a harmonious relationship with one of the samplers and inspectors of sumptuous banquets.

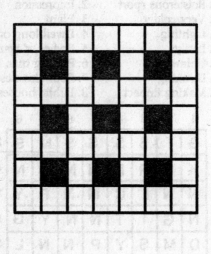

# Letter Change

*Solution 158*

The answer to each pair of clues is two words which differ by one letter only. For instance – To influence/to bring about (6) – answer: *affect/effect*.

(a) standing still/ writing materials (10)
(b) cleverly contrived /naïve (9)
(c) more speed/religious festival (6)
(d) indirect reference/deceptive appearance (8)
(e) unrefined/division of a meal (6)
(f) channel or pipe/direct (7)
(g) skilled/take up, as resolution (5)
(h) dim/pretence (5)
(i) abiding in/close at hand (8)
(j) berry/body of water (7)

# The Ultimate Counterfeit Coin Puzzle *Solution 120*

In a pile of twelve coins, there is a single counterfeit coin, which can be detected only by its weight. Using a balance scale, how can you find out in only three operations which coin is counterfeit and whether it is heavy or light?

You must enter each room once only in a continuous route and spell out a fifteen-letter word. You may enter the corridor as many times as you wish.

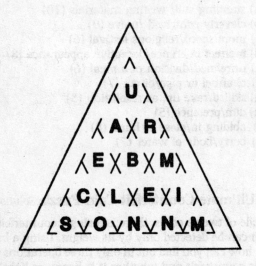

# Word Compasses

Place the letters in the correct boxes in each quadrant to obtain in each case two eight-letter words – one reading clockwise and the other anti-clockwise.

(a) The two words are synonyms.

NE: CEHT    SW: EEPS
SE: EIRS    NW: AARR

(b) The two words are antonyms.

NE: AAEG    SW: IIMN
SE: EIST    NW: CERT

# Double Acrostic

*Solution 75*

Each couplet provides the clue to a word. Solve the clues and list the five words. Two more words will be spelt out by the first and last letters of the five words.

> Tract of land green with grass,
> Happy place for lad and lass.

> I can prove it wasn't me,
> Was playing golf with Freddy Gee.

> Motive or logical point of view,
> Here's the rhyme now it's up to you.

> Claustrophobic thrusting pack,
> Several elbows in my back.

> Worry, torment, toil and trouble,
> Lots of hassle at the double.

# Division

*Solution 160*

Other than 57429 ÷ 6381, can you find two ways of arranging the numbers 1–9 to form a division sum which equals 9?

# Kangaroo Words

A kangaroo word is one which carries within it a smaller word which is a synonym; e.g. destruction – ruin. Find the synonyms within the following words – all letters are in the correct order.

1. BLOSSOMS  *BLOOMS*
2. EVACUATE  *VACATE*
3. ENCOURAGE
4. CALUMNIES
5. PERIMETER  *RIM*
6. RAPSCALLION  *RASCAL*
7. CURTAIL
8. PRATTLE
9. PERAMBULATE  *AMBLE*
10. JOVIALITY  *JOY*
11. REGULATES
12. SPLOTCHES  *SPOTS*
13. MATCHES
14. CONTAINER  *CAN*

**Which square is missing from the sequence – A, B, C or D?**

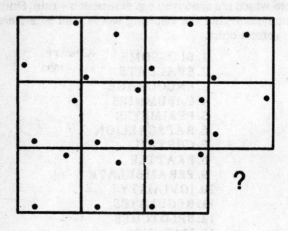

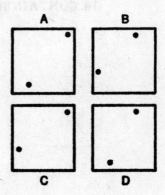

# Cross-alphabet

Insert the twenty-six letters of the alphabet once each only to form a crossword.

**Clues (no particular order)**

1. Wager
2. Cut grass
3. Denotes ownership
4. Calmness

5. Inflammation of throat
6. Box in mint
7. Knave at cards
8. Front part of helmet

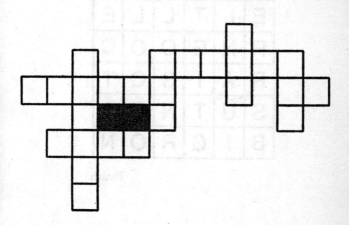

# Philosophy

Starting at the top left-hand corner, work horizontally, vertically or diagonally to find a quotation. Eight letters are redundant, and they form an anagram of the name of the philosopher whose words are quoted.

**Start**

| A | S | L | A | C | L |
|---|---|---|---|---|---|
| E | L | T | L | L | E |
| R | N | E | O | O | C |
| R | A | I | S | C | T |
| S | U | T | N | E | I |
| B | I | G | R | O | N |

**Finish**

66

## Something in Common

*Solution 148*

Solve the clues below. The answers have something in common.

1. A note
2. Legends
3. More coloured
4. Iranian monarchs
5. Spinner
6. Machine part
7. Canoe
8. Even
9. Municipal
10. Radio waves

## Missing Numbers

*Solution 51*

Fill in the missing numbers.

433/397/——
723/——/633
533/——/——

# Nursery Rhyme Crossword

*Solution 80*

*The clues to the crossword are hidden in the narrative. Find the clues, solve them and place the answers in the grid.*

There was an old woman who was one of the ugly nurses in authority, who liked to issue forth from a pair of Irish and Scottish Highland shoes of untanned leather.

She had so many children that she didn't know what to do. So she removes from a lorry some plants with stinging hairs and minced meat in cylindrical cases and makes some broth without any bread, whipped the children soundly and put them to bed, because she was apparently directed towards the outside type of woman and one of the well known perverts who loved cruelty.

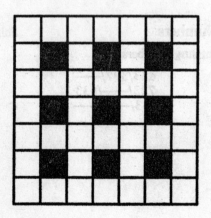

# Found in a Church

1. * A * E
2. * E * L *
3. * I * L *
4. * P * E
5. * M * U * A * O * Y
6. * R * N * E * T
7. * H * N * E *
8. * A * C * U * R *
9. * A * I * S * O * E
10. * I * E * I * O * D
11. * U * P * T
12. * M * O

# Probability Paradox

A ball is put in an empty bag. You don't know whether the ball is red or yellow. A second ball, which you know is red, is then put in the bag. A ball is then drawn out, and it proves to be red.

What are the chances that the ball remaining in the bag is also red?

# Missing Square

Which of the squares A–H is missing from the sequence?

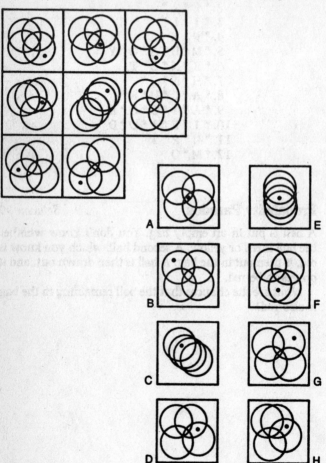

# Unscramble the Sequence

There is a logical way to get from the top left-hand square to the bottom right-hand one by moving from square to square horizontally, vertically or diagonally, and visiting each square once only. What is the sequence?

| 1 | 5 | 3 | 1 | 9 | 1 |
|---|---|---|---|---|---|
| 2 | 4 | 6 | 6 | 4 | 9 |
| 6 | 9 | 4 | 1 | 4 | 6 |
| 1 | 9 | 6 | 1 | 5 | 2 |
| 8 | 4 | 2 | 0 | 2 | 2 |
| 1 | 1 | 0 | 1 | 5 | 6 |

# Revolving

Complete the word in each column – they all end in 'R'. The scrambled letters in the section to the right of each column are an anagram of a word; *that* word will give a clue to the word you are trying to find, to fit in the column.

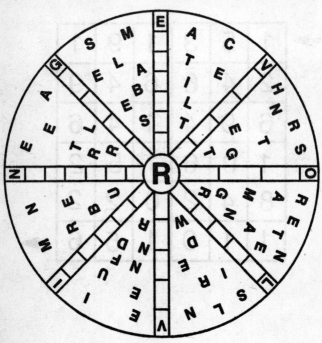

# Dominoes

Solution 78

Consider these five dominoes:

Now select one of these to complete the sequence.

A      B      C      D      E

## Collective Nouns

*Solution 154*

These twelve collective names have been mixed up. Rearrange them correctly.

| | |
|---|---|
| Business | of Butlers |
| Bevy | of Ducks |
| Down | of Sheldrake |
| Draught | of Flies |
| Erst | of Spiders |
| Cluster | of Starlings |
| Murmuration | of Turkeys |
| Sounder | of Moles |
| Badelyng | of Otters |
| Rafter | of Sheep |
| Doppin | of Boars |
| Labour | of Bees |

## Theme Anagram

*Solution 31*

Arrange the fourteen words into pairs which give anagrams of seven words. The seven words produced will have a linking theme. For instance, if the words *dial* and *than* appeared on the list, they could be paired to form an anagram of *Thailand*, and the theme could be 'countries'.

| | |
|---|---|
| BALL | PALE |
| CROON | RAIL |
| EACH | THE |
| GOAL | TONE |
| HELP | TRIAL |
| LOG | SHIRE |
| NEAT | WAY |

# Unique Features

Solution 86

Some numbers have a certain feature which does not occur with any other number. Three examples are given below.

A. What feature is peculiar to the number *four*?
B. What feature is peculiar to *twenty*?
C. What feature is peculiar to *forty*?

# Small Persons

Solution 157

Fill in the missing letters.

1. M I D G E T
2. P Y G M Y
3. * I * L * P * T * A *
4. * I * S * U * A *
5. * A * I * I *
6. * H * T
7. * H * I * P
8. * U * T
9. * O * U * C * L * S
10. * W * R *
11. * T * M *
12. T I C H

## Missing Number

Solution 10

What is the missing number?

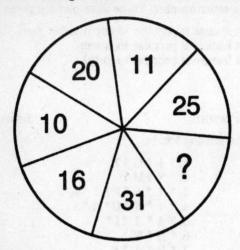

## Odd One Out

Solution 122

In each of the following, which word is the odd one out?

| A | B |
|---|---|
| OLD | SHOE |
| AWN | NARROW |
| GROVE | NUBILE |
| LACK | WHEAT |
| RANGE | STIPULATE |

# Collective Nouns

These twelve collective names have been mixed up. Rearrange them correctly.

| | | |
|---|---|---|
| Clowder | of | Sergeants |
| Rag | of | Widgeon |
| Unkindness | of | Whales |
| Company | of | Peacocks |
| Deceit | of | Cats |
| Horde | of | Ravens |
| Pod | of | Bears |
| Cast | of | Mules |
| Sloth | of | Colts |
| Subtilte | of | Lapwings |
| Baren | of | Falcons |
| Muster | of | Savages |

# Sequence

FUND
FOUND
UPROAR
AUDITOR

Find the logical progression in the sequence of words above, then supply a word in the English language which will complete the sequence.

## The Ultimate Shunting Puzzle     Solution 21

The train is 10 metres long and the coaches are each 5 metres long. All other dimensions other than those shown can be any length.

By shunting, you have to reverse the positions of coach A and coach B, and return the train to its starting point.

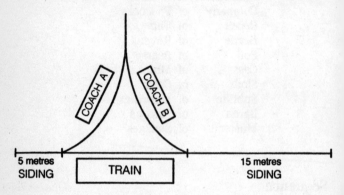

5 metres
SIDING

TRAIN

15 metres
SIDING

## Interesting Numbers     Solution 45

1. The square of 142857 is 20408122449. Why is this particularly interesting?

2. Which of these numbers is the odd one out?

4913
6859
5832
17576
19683

# Homonyms

Solution 142

Homonyms are words which have the same sound but different meanings – *hare* and *hair*, for instance. The answers to the twelve clues are all homonyms of cities or countries. *Example:* Bashful girl in Wyoming – Cheyenne (Shy Anne).

1. Mexican food in South America.
2. Coastal road in the Middle East.
3. Money in Scotland.
4. Parasitic insect in Asia.
5. Wildly foolish period in the Atlantic.
6. Wander about in Italy.
7. Attack coastal area in India.
8. Mammals in Britain.
9. One male in the Middle East.
10. Thick oil in Europe.
11. Secure singly in the Far East.
12. Regret prevailing craze in Europe.

# Connections

Insert the numbers 0 to 9 in the circles, so that for any particular circle the sum of the numbers in the circles connected directly to it equals the value corresponding to the number in that circle, as given in the list below.

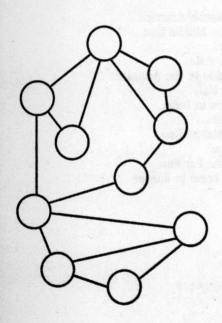

$$0 = 9$$
$$1 = 2$$
$$2 = 22$$
$$3 = 20$$
$$4 = 15$$
$$5 = 3$$
$$6 = 14$$
$$7 = 14$$
$$8 = 13$$
$$9 = 9$$

## Pair-words

Solution 56

Pair a word from list A with a word from list B, until you have ten matching pairs. There are two possible pairing words in list A with each word in list B and vice versa. There are two correct solutions.

| List A | List B |
|--------|--------|
| Misericord | Bards |
| Clay | Music |
| Wampum | Dagger |
| Eisteddfod | Brick |
| Cowrie | Apartment |
| Niche | Indian |
| Moccasin | Money |
| Stiletto | Vase |
| Mortar | Shoe |
| Chamber | Corner |
| Poets | Shells |

## Progression

Solution 149

Work out the answers to these clues. The answers follow a logical progression.

(a) Burdensome
(b) Double-dealing
(c) Suite of furniture
(d) Small forked instrument
(e) Ball game
(f) Type of gun

# Nursery Rhyme Crossword

*There are eight clues hidden in the narrative. When you have solved them, place the answers in their correct places in the grid.*

Jack and Jill were admiring the natural features of the district, playing places of incarceration and fabulous fire-breathing monsters, and listening to the transparent-winged, shrill-chirping insects, when they decided to fetch a pail of water. Jack's fall produced a spasmodic affliction of the muscles of the neck and bones enclosing the brain. Jill's tedious, tiresome, tumble, which upset her decorous manner and conduct, caused the water to move in an excited and disturbed manner.

# Quick Teasers

*Solution 47*

**A**

Mr Peters, Mr Edwards and Mr Roberts are playing a round of golf together. Halfway through the game Mr Peters remarks that he has just noticed that their Christian names are Peter, Edward and Robert. 'Yes,' says one of the others, 'I'd noticed that too, but none of us has the same surname as our own Christian name. For example, my first name is Robert.' What are the full names of the three golfers?

**B**

Five balls are placed in a hat. Each ball is marked with one of the letters K, O, O, T, Y. The balls are drawn out at random, one by one. What are the odds that they will be drawn out in the right order to spell out the name of a city in Japan?

# Double Meaning

*Solution 94*

Find a word in the English language which, without a change in pronunciation, has two directly contrary meanings.

> Thirty days have September,
> April, June and November;
> All the rest have thirty-one,
> Excepting February alone,
> Which has but twenty-eight days clear,
> And twenty-nine in each leap year.

This is perhaps the best-known of all mnemonics, but there are many more besides, some already known, others which will be of your own invention. Which direction is East and which is West are easily remembered by thinking of the word 'we'. Stalactites hang from the ceiling and stalagmites rise from the ground. The difference between dromedary and Bactrian camels becomes evident when laying their initial letters on their side: 'D' (one hump), 'B' (two humps).

Below are four more examples of mnemonics. Can you say what each will enable you to remember?

1. Richard of York gained battles in vain.
2. Mother very eagerly made jam sandwiches, under no protest.
3. No point letting your trousers slip half-way.
4.        Now I know a rhyme excelling,
   In hidden words and magic spelling,
   Wranglers perhaps deploring,
   For me its nonsense isn't boring.

# Word Track

Solution 114

Track from letter to letter horizontally, vertically or diagonally to find a sixteen-letter word.

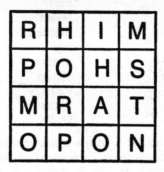

# Nexus

Solution 64

Each pair of words leads to another word, with the number of letters indicated by the dots. Complete words 18–30 so that you arrive at the final word, 'Nexus'.

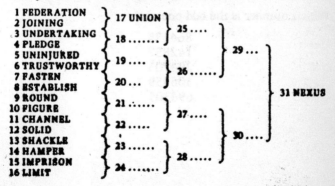

1 FEDERATION
2 JOINING
3 UNDERTAKING
4 PLEDGE
5 UNINJURED
6 TRUSTWORTHY
7 FASTEN
8 ESTABLISH
9 ROUND
10 FIGURE
11 CHANNEL
12 SOLID
13 SHACKLE
14 HAMPER
15 IMPRISON
16 LIMIT

17 UNION
18 .......
19 ....
20 ...
21 ......
22 .....
23 ......
24 .......

25 ....
26 ......
27 ....
28 .....

29 ...
30 ....

31 NEXUS

## Pair-words

| List A | List B |
|--------|--------|
| Ammunition | Phoenix |
| Bridge | Pork |
| Guinea | Desert |
| Arizona | Blackbird |
| Bird | Pig |
| Wampum | Rocket |
| Porcine | Money |
| Oasis | Railway |
| Train | Water |
| Pie | Shells |

Pair a word from list A with a word from list B until you have ten matched pairs. Each word in list A has two possible pair-words in List B. Each word in list B has two possible pair-words in list A. There are two correct solutions.

## Odd Numbers

Which number is the odd one out?

864135
142857
294705
306459
694305

# Trios

*Solution 66*

Some nine-letter words consist of three three-letter words, for example, *woebegone/woe-beg-one*. You have to use all the three-letter words below to form five nine-letter words.

| Ate | Bed | Den | Off | Sea |
|-----|-----|-----|-----|-----|
| Bar | Bit | Did | One | Son |
| Bat | Can | Her | Rid | Sun |

# Find Another Word

*Solution 26*

In each case consider the words in list 1, and then select one word from list 2 to add to them. The connection is the same in all four pairs of lists.

**A**
List 1: arms, car, walk, real, board
List 2: legs, trolley, track, false, deep

**B**
List 1: some, out, writing, bill
List 2: others, in, holdall, bag, till, bank

**C**
List 1: write, hand, stand, take, ground
List 2: calm, fine, seating, valid, charge

**D**
List 1: over, table, out, key, coat
List 2: gate, stile, road, path, walk

# Square Words

Travel clockwise round the perimeter and finish at the centre square to spell out the nine-letter words. Each word starts at a corner square. You supply the missing letters.

# Wot! No Vowels

Move horizontally, vertically or diagonally from square to square to find five words, starting in the top left-hand corner and finishing in the bottom right. Use each square once only, and use all the letters.

START

| G | S | T | H | M |
|---|---|---|---|---|
| Y | Y | P | Y | T |
| S | M | Y | H | R |
| Y | H | T | R | Y |
| L | P | H | S | T |

FINISH

TRYST

GYPSY.

## Swap Around

Solution 33

Find the next square in the sequence.

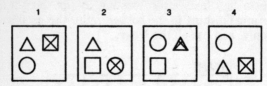

Choose from these squares.

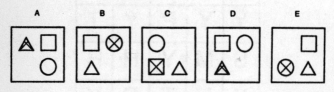

## Cheerfulness

Solution 84

Find the missing letters for these words, which are connected with cheerfulness.

1. *A*G*T*R
2. *I*A*I*Y
3. *L*E
4. *E*I*Y
5. *E*R*M*N*
6. *R*E*I*E*S
7. *O*N*I*E*S
8. *P*I*I*M
9. *A*E*Y
10. *B*L*I*N*E
11. *I*T*
12. *O*L*T*

# Added Difficulty

In these two sequences, which is the odd one out? 'I' has a different answer from 'II'.

**I**

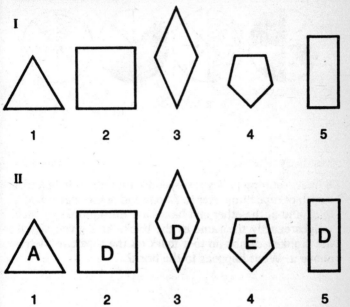

1     2     3     4     5

**II**

1     2     3     4     5

# Odd One Out

*Solution 55*

Which is the odd one out?

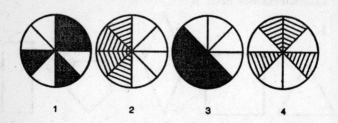

1      2      3      4

# Monkey Puzzle

*Solution 125*

A freely rotating pulley is suspended from the ceiling and a length of rope hung over it. At one end of the rope is tied a brick and at the other end hangs a trained monkey which weighs exactly the same as the brick. At a given signal, the monkey climbs up to a mark on the rope two metres above it. What happens to the brick?

# Missing Square

Find the missing square.

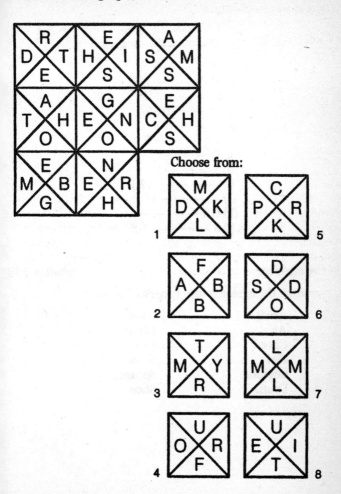

Choose from:

1

2

3

4

5

6

7

8

# Eat and Drink

Solution 128

Insert the name of something to eat or drink to complete these words. *Examples:*

$$— — — R: Tear$$
$$P — — — —: Price$$

- (a) F — — — — P
- (b) P Y — — — A S
- (c) B — — — — E D
- (d) — — — D L E
- (e) — — — T Y
- (f) E N — — — E
- (g) S — — — K
- (h) S — — — E
- (i) — — — — A R D
- (j) — — — — L
- (k) G R — — — —
- (l) S — — — — L E

# Categorize

Solution 130

Arrange these words into groups of three.

| | |
|---|---|
| Anvil | Forge |
| Arc | Horse |
| Chord | Key |
| Clef | Scale |
| Cochlea | Secant |
| Drum | Shoe |

# Pyramid

*Solution 152*

You must enter each room only once in a continuous route and spell out a fifteen-letter word. You may enter the corridor as many times as you wish.

# Hyphenated Words

*Solution 57*

These segments are all extracted from the middle of hyphenated words. You have to find the words. *Example:* EY-PU – MONKEY-PUZZLE.

| | |
|---|---|
| ON-HU | EP-DI |
| SY-GO | AT-TR |
| TH-EA | UR-PO |
| HT-WA | IN-RA |
| EN-PE | NT-BL |
| US-PO | LY-CO |
| ET-MA | DY-GU |

# Nursery Rhyme Crossword

*Concealed in the narrative are eight clues. All you have to do is to solve them and then fit the answers into the grid.*

Wee Willie Winkie travelled with rapidity of movement through the town, upstairs and downstairs in his loose silk or cotton trousers, slowed down to close and open his eyes at a fat, oily, greasy, muttonheaded, thickheaded dunderhead, but longed and craved to wander at random without help or assistance.

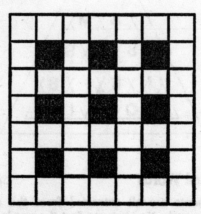

# Word Power

Answers will be found, letters in order, in the grid. Use each letter once only.

1. Bracket candlestick. (6)
2. Sailor. (7)
3. House lizard. (5)
4. Of a bear. (6)
5. Enlarged thyroid gland. (6)
6. Mixture of collie, sheep-dog and greyhound. (7)
7. Of nape of neck. (6)
8. Whirlpool. (9)
9. Cushioned seat. (7)
10. Wheel of life. (8)
11. Part of horse's leg. (7)
12. Ring of twisted rope. (7)

*Example:* 1. Sconce

| O | M | Z | G | L | F | U | G | R |
|---|---|---|---|---|---|---|---|---|
| G | M | S | N | T | U | E | O | U |
| U | T | R | A | A | M | E | E | O |
| I | T | R | C | O | T | E | C | M |
| E | E | C | R | C | M | T | S | L |
| O | H | O | L | S | H | I | T | T |
| L | E | K | R | O | A | A | N | P |
| O | O | C | R | L | N | R | O | N |
| T | T | E | M | E | C | E | K | E |

# All Change

What comes next in this sequence?

Choose from these.

A          B          C          D

# Word Circle

In the example, a ring of six-letter words, each overlapping by two letters, is divided into two-letter groups and arranged in alphabetical order. AN, ED, GL, IT, OR, PH *gives the answer:* ANGLED, EDITOR, ORPHAN.

Now try to unscramble the letter-pairs below, to find a circle of eight six-letter words.

AD, AD, CO, ER, GA, HE, LE, MI, MY, NE, ON, OR, RE, RI, ST, UR

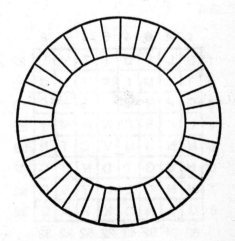

# I-frame

Each horizontal and vertical line includes the consonants of a word which can be completed by adding only a number of 'I' vowels.

The two-figure number at the end of each line indicates the number of consonants and vowels. For instance, 62 indicates 6 consonants and 2 'I' vowels.

Each letter in the grid is used only once, and all letters must be used.

**Across**
1. Perfectionist
2. Bantu warriors
3. Virtually contained
4. Flower
5. Requesting
   courteously
6. Numeral
7. Mischievously
8. Stiff

**Down**
1. Illuminations
2. Lazily
3. Stay at wicket
4. Illegal
5. Bird
6. Innate impulse
7. Half a semibreve
8. Of citizens

|   | 1 | 2 | 3 | 4 | 5 | 6 | 7 | 8 |    |
|---|---|---|---|---|---|---|---|---|----|
| 1 | S | L | S | D | T | T | Y | L | 62 |
| 2 | T | Y | M | L | P | T | N | C | 22 |
| 3 | G | P | N | M | T | S | L | C | 53 |
| 4 | L | S | R | C | W | N | M | V | 22 |
| 5 | N | N | N | G | V | C | T | N | 53 |
| 6 | H | D | G | T | D | N | T | C | 32 |
| 7 | M | H | G | L | L | Y | S | P | 62 |
| 8 | G | L | N | D | K | R | M | G | 32 |

62 31 52 43 22 62 32 32

# Progression

Consider these figures:

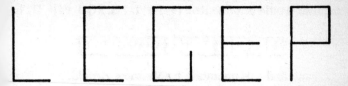

Which of these continues the sequence?

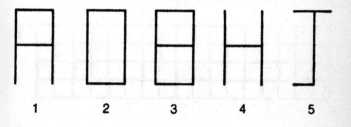

# Piecemeal Quotation

A quotation has been divided up into three-letter groups and arranged in alphabetical order. For example, 'find the quote' would be presented: (4-3-5) DTH, EQU, FIN, OTE.

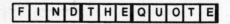

Now find this quotation by Matthew Arnold.
(2-3-3-4-2-4-10-5-2-3-5-3-4-2-4-3-2-4-4).

AVE, ELI, ERE, EWO, FAC, GTH, HEM, ILI, KEB, KET, OIN, OMA, ORD, OTH, REN, RKW, SFO, TIE, TOH, UND, USF, UTT, WEA.

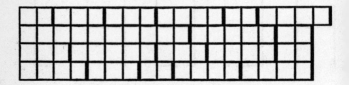

# Sequence

Continue this sequence.

7, 41, 12, 82, 53, 24, —

## Swap Round

Solution 58

Change the numbers to letters to find four six-letter words.

123456
623451
423156
426153

## Spirals

Solution 48

Find the next figure in this sequence.

1

2

3

Choose from:

A

B

C

D

# Pair-words

*Solution 92*

Pair a word from list A with a word from list B, until you have ten matching pairs. There are two possible pairing words in list A with each word in list B and vice versa. There are two correct solutions.

| | |
|---|---|
| Bidonville | Euclid |
| Straw | Cathedral |
| Diocese | Oil-drum |
| Boa | Fish |
| Pythagoras | Town |
| Jelly | Hat |
| Petroleum | Bishop |
| Shako | Tuscan |
| City | Snake |
| Fibonacci | Petrolatum |
| Eel | Diagonal |
| Fianchetto | Plume |

# Letter Omission

*Solution 127*

The answers to each pair of clues are two words which differ by the omission of one letter only. *Example:* gun/churchman (6/5) – cannon/canon.

1. Dislike intensely/unwilling (6/5)
2. To rule/narrow strap (5/4)
3. Decree/military stores (9/8)
4. Apparel/fabrics (7/6)
5. Honour as holy/permit (6/5)
6. Earnest request/dismay (6/5)
7. Shuffle/change (6/5)
8. Manner of walking/small island (4/3)
9. Gape/beard of corn (4/3)
10. Establish/resources (5/4)

# Nursery Rhyme Crossword

*Concealed in the narrative which follows are eight clues. All that you have to do is to solve them and fit the answers into the grid.*

Sing a song of sixpence, played on a small egg-shaped terracotta wind instrument, pocket full of rye, cut by persons wielding sickles, four and twenty red-legged black crows, accosted with salutations by cooks, cut up with carving knives and carving forks, immersed in boiling water and baked in a pie.

I keep in undecided or inoperative state this handwritten literary work until publication.

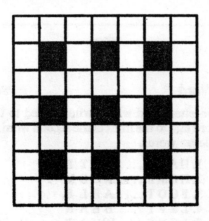

## The Plank

Solution 32

You have a two-metre plank of wood, of uniform width and thickness throughout, and weighing exactly 10 kg. You make three cuts as shown to divide the plank into four equal pieces of equal weight.

How much does each piece weigh?

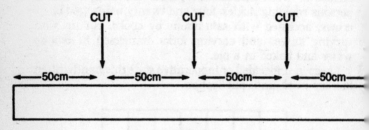

## Middle Word

Solution 98

Find a four-letter word which when added to the end of the first word and to the front of the second word, produces two eight-letter words.

1. HARD .... MATE
2. HOME .... ROOM
3. FOOT .... ABLE
4. LEFT .... BEAR
5. LONE .... WHAT
6. GAME .... CROW
7. CHAR .... HOLE
8. BUZZ .... PLAY
9. LOVE .... LIST
10. BACK .... BOWL

A cryptogram is a straightforward code in which each letter of the alphabet has been replaced by another. Start by solving the cryptogram that follows.

> JHBX, AEHJ FMY IDH KHLODRNRJQ
> I LEIVH, MD LMYJK, MD XRJX;
> KMJ'X LXIXH XEH GIXXHD VUIRJUF,
> NYX VYX RX RJ I ERJX;
> IJK UHIDJ XM UMMT IX IUU XERJQL
> ARXE I LMDX MP GHJXIU LWYRJX.
>                – UHARL OIDDMUU.

Now try to find a keyed phrase (5, 3, 6) connected with the cryptogram. Under each letter of plain text (line 1) write its encoded form (line 2). Then, under each letter of code text (line 3) write its plain text form (line 4). You will find that most of line 4 is in alphabetical order – the letters which are not are those making up the key phrase. They appear in their correct order, but of course repeated letters have been omitted and must be replaced; a little imagination is needed to work out the hidden phrase. For instance, *anpledy* would be all that would appear of an apple a day'.

| 1 | A | B | C | D | E | F | G | H | I | J | K | L | M | N | O | P | Q | R | S | T | U | V | W | X | Y | Z |
|---|---|---|---|---|---|---|---|---|---|---|---|---|---|---|---|---|---|---|---|---|---|---|---|---|---|---|
| 2 |   |   |   |   |   |   |   |   |   |   |   |   |   |   |   |   |   |   |   |   |   |   |   |   |   |   |
| 3 | A | B | C | D | E | F | G | H | I | J | K | L | M | N | O | P | Q | R | S | T | U | V | W | X | Y | Z |
| 4 |   |   |   |   |   |   |   |   |   |   |   |   |   |   |   |   |   |   |   |   |   |   |   |   |   |   |

# Odd Ones Out

*Solution 87*

Which are the odd words out in these two lists?

| A | B |
|---|---|
| MILE | SAGE |
| RACED | SASH |
| AMPLE | SAXE |
| OPEN | SCAN |
| PANES | SCAR |
| | SEAR |

# Heteronyms

*Solution 22*

Heteronyms are two words or phrases with the same spelling but different pronunciations and meanings. For instance, *remarkable/incapable* (7/3,4) – *notable/not able*.

1. Air in motion/meander (4/4)
2. Hold up/sip strong red wine (7/3,4)
3. Make reparation/in complete accord (5/2,3)
4. Pull apart/fluid in eye (4/4)
5. Large book/in my direction (4/2,2)
6. Very small/record of proceedings (6/6)
7. Give/university teacher did feed (6/3,3)
8. Carved rocks/most solemn persons (11/7,4)
9. Propel boat/disturbance (3/3)
10. Has arrived/not in any place (3,4/7)
11. Limb extremity/inscription (3,3/6)
12. Victory at the present time/blow free of chaff (3,3/6)

# Solutions

## 1. Number Crossword

*page 20*

| P | E | T | I | M | A | N | Y | D |
|---|---|---|---|---|---|---|---|---|
| C | E | N | C | I | R | E | N | D |
| H | I | D | T | O | S | E | I | E |
| O | D | H | O | O | M | A | B | F |
| P | A | A | P | M | M | E | A | R |
| P | B | S | O | O | E | B | T | A |
| E | I | C | N | T | R | T | E | W |
| D | E | D | E | B | I | T | E | D |
| R | O | T | C | E | L | F | E | R |

## 2. Typewriter

*page 24*

Typewriter.

## 3. Nines

*page 38*

| 7 | 2 | 6 | 8 | 4 |
|---|---|---|---|---|
| 3 | 6 | 1 | 5 | 3 |
| 9 | 2 | 8 | 3 | 5 |
| 4 | 8 | 3 | 1 | 2 |
| 4 | 9 | 9 | 1 | 4 |

111

## 4. Word Search

| | |
|---|---|
| 1. Hubris | 13. Tea |
| 2. Ganoid | 14. Twig |
| 3. Kelpie | 15. Hire |
| 4. Spelter | 16. Girl |
| 5. Kraken | 17. Drew |
| 6. Keep | 18. Ewe |
| 7. Noble | 19. Fun |
| 8. Tulle | 20. Bag |
| 9. Girth | 21. Ken |
| 10. Range | 22. Ark |
| 11. Proof | 23. Gore |
| 12. Betel | 24. Tin |

## 5. Odd Numbers

306459 – in the others the number formed by the first three digits added to that formed by the last three gives a total of 999.

## 6. Sequence

Typewriter keys/alphabetical sequence : 21.

| 17 | 23 | 5 | 18 | 20 | 25 | 21 |
|---|---|---|---|---|---|---|
| Q | W | E | R | T | Y | U |

## 7. Connections

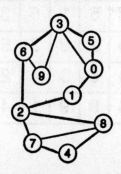

## 8. Pair-words

Canaster – Canasta – Cards
Cards – Kibitzer – Spectator
Spectator – Watcher – Bird
Bird – Thrush – Lark
Lark – Sky – Azure
Azure – Green – Orange
Orange – Segment – Arc
Arc – Joan – Rose
Rose – Bud – Leaf
Leaf – Tobacco – Canaster

## 9. Vowel

*page 28*

H.

## 10. Missing Number

*page 76*

13. Start at 10 and jump one space each time, adding 1, then 2, then 3, then 4, then 5, then 6.

## 11. Philosophy

*page 66*

All learning is but recollection' – Socrates.

## 12. Work It Out

*page 46*

51 – so that the three numbers in each circle add up to 100.

## 13. Nursery Rhyme Crossword *page 36*

|   |   |   |   |   |   |
|---|---|---|---|---|---|
| R | E | C | L | U | S | E |

```
R E C L U S E
E   A   N   N
S T R A I N T
I   A   F   A
D E V I O U S
E   A   R   I
D Y N A M O S
```

## 14. Eight-pointed Star *page 22*

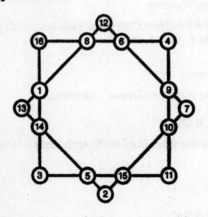

## 15. Conditional *page 30*
Flag.

## 16. Pair-words

*page 5*

Dog – Canine – Mandibles
Mandibles – Jaws – Shark
Shark – Mackerel – Perch
Perch – Passerine – Thrush
Thrush – Fungus – Mushroom
Mushroom – Toadstool – Umbrella
Umbrella – Rain – Nimbus
Nimbus – Halo – Moon
Moon – Planet – Star
Star – Sirius – Dog

## 17. Children

*page 49*

Two, five, eight, eleven, fourteen, seventeen, twenty, twenty-three and twenty-six. The mother is forty-eight.

## 18. Unscramble the Sequence

*page 71*

Proceed via square numbers – 1, 4, 9, 16, 25, 36, 49, 64, 81, 100, 121, 144, 169, 196, 225, 256.

## 19. Word Power

*page 97*

1. Sconce
2. Matelot
3. Gecko
4. Ursine
5. Goitre
6. Lurcher
7. Nuchal
8. Maelstrom
9. Ottoman
10. Zoetrope
11. Fetlock
12. Grummet

## 20. Catch a Fish

*page 53*

1. Sole
2. Perch
3. Flounder
4. Bass
5. Pike
6. Carp

## 21. The Ultimate Shunting Puzzle page 78

Train to 15-metre siding, collect coach B. Back to 15-metre siding, leave B in 5-metre siding. Back to 15-metre siding, up to top, pick up A and push down on to B in 5-metre siding. Reverse up to top. Drop B in its original place and come back up with A to the top. Take A to 5-metre siding and leave. Reverse to top, collect B and reverse to top. Leave B in A's original position. Reverse train and go across to 15-metre siding. Push A up to B's original position and return train to starting-point.

## 22. Heteronyms page 108

1. Wind/wind
2. Support/sup port
3. Atone/at one
4. Tear/tear
5. Tome/to me
6. Minute/minute
7. Donate/don ate
8. Gravestones/gravest ones
9. Row/row
10. Now here/nowhere
11. Leg end/legend
12. Win now/winnow

## 23. Letter Search page 32

1. B, 2. E, 3. L, 4. P

## 24. Squares page 55

Yes.

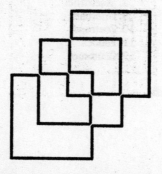

### 25. Sixes

*page 48*

*Latchspring* and *Catchphrase*.

### 26. Find Another Word

*page 87*

A. Track. All words can be prefixed with *side*.
B. Bag. All can be prefixed with *hand*.
C. Charge. All can be prefixed with *under*.
D. Stile. All can be prefixed with *turn*.

### 27. Logic

*page 64*

B: the top right-hand dot visits four positions three times each, and the bottom left-hand dot visits three positions four times each.

### 28. Odd One

*page 14*

*UP* – the remaining words form a new word when the last letter is repeated.

### 29. Nursery Rhyme Crossword

*page 96*

## 30. Killer

page 16

Arthur

## 31. Theme Anagram

page 74

Elephant (help, neat), antelope (pale, tone), gorilla (rail, log), rhinoceros (croon, shire), wallaby (ball, way), cheetah (each, the), alligator (trial, goal).

## 32. The Plank

page 106

Slightly less than 2.5 kg, because some weight is lost in the form of sawdust.

## 33. Swap Around

page 90

B. The symbol which contained the cross always moves to the opposite corner, and the symbol which occupied that corner moves across to the previously unoccupied space, taking the cross with it.

## 34. Candles

page 35

They have been burning for three hours.

## 35. Nursery Rhyme Crossword

page 3

## 36. Word Search

*page 27*

1. Assagai
2. Trivet
3. Saluki
4. Siesta
5. Radii
6. Sap
7. Aspects
8. Dares
9. Regal
10. Lager
11. Taker
12. Argued
13. Tall
14. Speaker
15. Ink
16. Case
17. Seen
18. Sen
19. Asp
20. Ruins
21. Lei
22. Else

## 37. Fruit

*page 8*

1. AVOCADO
2. CRANBERRY
3. PEACH
4. HUCKLEBERRY
5. MELON/LEMON
6. RASPBERRY
7. PRUNE
8. LOGANBERRY
9. CANTALOUPE
10. BANANA/PAPAYA
11. MANDARIN
12. APRICOT

## 38. Nursery Rhyme Crossword

*page 23*

| | | | | | | |
|---|---|---|---|---|---|---|
| P | E | L | I | C | A | N |
| R | | A | | H | | E |
| O | U | T | S | I | Z | E |
| M | | T | | M | | D |
| I | N | I | T | I | A | L |
| S | | C | | N | | E |
| E | M | E | R | G | E | D |

## 39. Antigrams

*page 37*

1. Militarism
2. Legislation
3. Infection
4. Protectionism
5. Commendation
6. Revelations
7. Anarchists
8. Adversaries
9. Enormity
10. Desecration

## 40. Overlapping Words

*page 54*

(a) Testament
(b) Staunchest
(c) Tessellate
(d) Underground.

## 41. Spots

*page 12*

## 42. Nursery Rhyme Crossword

*page 47*

## 43. Missing Square

*page 70*

C: the dot appears in a total of six circles in each horizontal, vertical and corner-to-corner line.

### 44. Fish
*page 39*

Trout, perch, cod, plaice, haddock, mackerel, salmon, sturgeon.

### 45. Interesting Numbers
*page 78*

1. 20408 + 122449 = 142857
2. 6859. They are all cube numbers, but in all the others the sum of the digits is equal to the cube root.

### 46. Kangaroo Words
*page 63*

1. Blooms
2. Vacate
3. Urge
4. Lies
5. Rim
6. Rascal
7. Cut
8. Prate
9. (R)amble
10. Joy
11. Rules
12. Spots
13. Mates
14. Can/Tin

### 47. Quick Teasers
*page 83*

A. Mr Peters must be Edward because the man who spoke last is Robert and he is not Mr Peters. Therefore the others are Robert Edwards and Peter Roberts.
B. The balls can be drawn out in 120 different ways, that is, 5! or 5 × 4 × 3 × 2 × 1. As two of the balls carry the same letter, and it is possible to spell out the names of *two* cities, Tokyo and Kyoto, with the letters, the odds are 116 to 4, or 29/1.

### 48. Spirals
*page 103*

B: each spiral moves through ninety degrees each time. The outer and inner spirals move clockwise, and the middle spiral moves anticlockwise.

### 49. Needle
*page 5*

$$\frac{1}{Pi}$$

## 50. Piano

*page 12*

*With hyphens.*
CABBAGE-BED
BEADED-EDGE
FACE-BEDDED

*Without hyphens*
BEBEDDED
BEDEAFED
CABBAGED
DEBAGGED
DEBADGED

## 51. Missing Numbers

*page 67*

433/397/208
723/681/633
533/488/232

In each horizontal line of numbers, you work out the product of the digits of each number and subtract it from that number to obtain the next one. So $4 \times 3 \times 3 = 36$; $433 - 36 = 397$; $3 \times 9 \times 7 = 189$; $397 - 189 = 208$.

## 52. Added Difficulty

*page 91*

I. 5 – all the other figures have all sides equal.
II. 1 – in all the other figures the position of the letter in the alphabet coincides with the number of sides of the figure in which it is contained.

## 53. Alphabet.

*page 7*

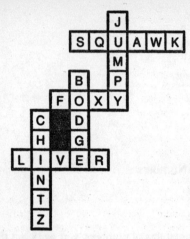

## 54. E-frame

*page 26*

| Across | Down |
|--------|------|
| 1. Berets | 1. Wrens |
| 2. Zebec | 2. Defer |
| 3. Geezer | 3. Errs |
| 4. Renew | 4. Screw |
| 5. Peter | 5. Shrew |
| 6. Teetered | 6. Eschew |
| 7. Scheme | 7. Eddy |

## 55. Odd One Out

*page 92*

1 – in the others each black or lined section is always opposite a white section.

### 56. Pair-words

*page 81*

Dagger – Misericord – Apartment
Apartment – Chamber – Music
Music – Eisteddfod – Bards
Bards – Poets – Corner
Corner – Niche – Vase
Vase – Clay – Brick
Brick – Mortar – Shells
Shells – Cowrie – Money
Money – Wampum – Indian
Indian – Moccasin – Shoe
Shoe – Stiletto – Dagger

### 57. Hyphenated Words

*page 95*

Lion-hunter, easy-going, moth-eaten, tight-wad/weight-watcher, hen-pecked, hocus-pocus, cabinet-maker, sheep-dip, hat-trick, four-poster, curtain-raiser, point-blank, molly-coddle, hurdy-gurdy.

### 58. Swap Round

*page 103*

Danger, ranged, gander, garden.

### 59. Can You Help?

*page 45*

Call the longest side $x$. Call the shortest side $y$.

Add to the answer $\left(\dfrac{x + y}{2}\right)\left(\dfrac{x - y}{2}\right)$

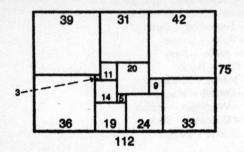

EUPHORIAL or EQUATION Number of letters increases by one, and a new vowel is added each time.

1 – the number of right-angles in the figure increases by one every time.

## 64. Nexus

*page 85*

```
17 UNION    ⎫
18 PROMISE  ⎬ 25 BOND    ⎫
19 SAFE     ⎫           ⎬ 29 TIE   ⎫
20 FIX      ⎬ 26 SECURE ⎭          ⎬ 31 NEXUS
21 CIRCLE   ⎫                      ⎪
22 SOUND    ⎬ 27 RING   ⎫          ⎭
23 FETTER   ⎫           ⎬ 30 LINK
24 CONFINE  ⎬ 28 CHAIN  ⎭
```

## 65. Logic

*page 6*

B.

## 66. Trios

*page 87*

Candidate, barbitone, sunbather, bedridden, offseason.

## 67. Highest Number

*page 29*

We can make it as high as we wish to infinity in the following form:

$((((( 1111 !) !) !) !) !) ! ........$

## 68. Pronouns

*page 49*

Ushers – us, she, he, her, hers.

## 69. Collective Nouns

*page 35*

| | | | |
|---|---|---|---|
| Observance of | Hermits | Colony | of Rabbits |
| Melody | of Harpers | Trip | of Sheep |
| Exaltation | of Larks | Husk | of Hares |
| Siege | of Cranes | Tribe | of Goats |
| Watch | of Nightingales | Kennel | of Raches |
| Parliament of | Owls | Cry | of Hounds |

### 70. Revolving
*page 72*

Espalier (lattice), vigour (strength), order (arrangement), lurcher (swindler), vulgar (unrefined), integer (number), narrator (relater), gather (assemble).

### 71. Three Cryptograms
*page 10*

1. A conference is a gathering of important people who singly can do nothing but together can decide that nothing can be done – Fred Allen
2. Political skill . . . the ability to foretell what is going to happen tomorrow, next week, next month and next year. And to have the ability afterwards to explain why it didn't happen – Sir Winston Churchill
3. A synonym is a word you use when you can't spell the word you first thought of – Burt Bacharach

### 72. Ferry
*page 39*

1. I take the Tiger across.
2. I return alone.
3. I take the Hippo across.
4. I return with the Tiger.
5. I take the Lamb across.
6. I return alone.
7. I take the Tiger across.

### 73. Africa
*page 21*

| | |
|---|---|
| Algeria | Mali |
| Ghana | Nigeria |
| Kenya | Sudan |
| Liberia | Uganda |
| Libya | Zaire |

### 74. Pair-words page 86

Blackbird – Pie – Pork
Pork – Porcine – Pig
Pig – Guinea – Money
Money – Wampum – Shells
Shells – Ammunition – Rocket
Rocket – Train – Railway
Railway – Bridge – Water
Water – Oasis – Desert
Desert – Arizona – Phoenix
Phoenix – Bird – Blackbird

### 75. Double Acrostic page 62

| | | |
|---|---|---|
| M | EADO | W |
| A | LIB | I |
| R | EASO | N |
| C | ROW | D |
| H | ARAS | S |

### 76. Word Circle page 99

Ermine, neuron, oncost, stormy, myriad, adhere, regale, leader.

### 77. Eleven page 33

If the sums of alternate numbers are equal it divides by eleven.
For instance, 4762153.

### 78. Dominoes page 73

B – to complete every possible pairing of the four different symbols.

## 79. Piecemeal Quotation

*page 102*

| W E | A R E | N O | T | H E R E | T O | H A | V E |
|---|---|---|---|---|---|---|---|
| F A | C I L I T I E S | F O U N D | U S |
| F O R | D O I N G | T H E | W O R K | W E |
| L I K E | B U T | T O | M A K E | T H E M |

## 80. Nursery Rhyme Crossword

*page 68*

## 81. Missing Square

*page 93*

8. To complete this message, reading along each horizontal line of letters: READ THIS MESSAGE THEN CHOOSE NUMBER EIGHT.

130

## 82. Nursery Rhyme Crossword

*page 82*

## 83. No Hyphens

*page 13*

DEFy
STUmp
caNOPy
thiRSTy
HIJacker

## 84. Cheerfulness

*page 90*

1. Laughter
2. Hilarity
3. Glee
4. Levity
5. Merriment
6. Breeziness
7. Bounciness
8. Optimism
9. Gaiety
10. Ebullience
11. Mirth
12. Jollity

## 85. Sequence

*page 102*

94 – the numbers of the 7-times table reversed.

## 86. Unique Features

*page 75*

A. It is spelt with the corresponding number of letters.
B. It starts with the corresponding number letter of the alphabet.
C. Its letters are in alphabetical order.

## 87. Odd Ones Out

*page 108*

A. Open. The rest are tree anagrams – lime, cedar, maple, aspen.
B. Sash. In the others the letter 's' can be moved to the end of the word to form a new word in the plural.

## 88. Number

*page 21*

840.

## 89. I-frame

*page 57*

| Across | Down |
|--------|------|
| 1. Ibis | 1. Inching |
| 2. Jinks | 2. Imprint |
| 3. Icily | 3. Iris |
| 4. Igniting | 4. Insist |
| 5. Idly | 5. Impis |
| 6. Illicit | 6. Innings |
| 7. Imbibing | 7. Infinity |
| 8. Impinging | 8. Inns |

## 90. Routes

*page 9*

2,704,156.

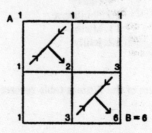

Each number is generated by adding the diagonal numbers above.

## 91. Square

*page 28*

Magnetism.

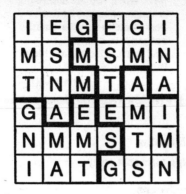

## 92. Pair-words

*page 104*

Fish – Eel – Snake
Petrolatum – Jelly – Fish
Oil-drum – Petroleum – Petrolatum
Town – Bidonville – Oil-drum
Cathedral – City – Town
Bishop – Diocese – Cathedral
Diagonal – Fianchetto – Bishop
Euclid – Pythagoras – Diagonal
Tuscan – Fibonacci – Euclid
Hat – Straw – Tuscan
Plume – Shako – Hat
Snake – Boa – Plume

## 93. Cryptokey page 107

> Next, when you are describing
> A shape, or sound, or tint;
> Don't state the matter plainly,
> But put it in a hint;
> And learn to look at all things
> With a sort of mental squint.
>          – Lewis Carroll

Message keyed: R H Y M E A N D S O (*Rhyme and reason*).

## 94. Double Meaning page 83

Cleave – to cling to/to split away.

## 95. Collective Nouns page 77

| | |
|---|---|
| Subtilte | of Sergeants |
| Company | of Widgeon |
| Pod | of Whales |
| Muster | of Peacocks |
| Clowder | of Cats |
| Unkindness | of Ravens |
| Sloth | of Bears |
| Baren | of Mules |
| Rag | of Colts |
| Deceit | of Lapwings |
| Cast | of Falcons |
| Horde | of Savages |

## 96. Triangles page 14

111.

## 97. Letters

page 46

The shapes in which the letters are placed have the same symmetrical property as the letters themselves.

AHIM – laterally symmetric
BCDEK – vertically symmetric
OX – radially symmetric
NSZ – rotated symmetric
FGJLPQR – asymmetric
TUVWY – laterally symmetric

## 98. Middle Word

page 106

1. Ship
2. Sick/Ward/Work
3. Wear/Mark/Work
4. Over
5. Some
6. Cock
7. Coal
8. Word
9. Sick
10. Hand/Wash

## 99. Probability Paradox

page 69

Two chances in three.

Call the balls which may be put in the bag first *R1* and *Y*, and call the red ball which you see go in *R2*. After the red ball has been taken out, there are three possibilities:

(a) *R1* still in the bag, *R2* outside;
(b) *R2* still in the bag, *R1* outside;
(c) *Y* still in the bag, *R2* outside.

## 100. Middle Words

page 4

1. Bell
2. Her
3. Gain
4. Out
5. Ant
6. Haul
7. Get
8. Mat
9. Us
10. Son
11. Ton
12. Ant
13. Here
14. Act
15. Less
16. Or
17. Wry
18. Lace
19. Dock
20. Form

## 101. Triangles

*page 24*

59.

## 102. Pair-words

*page 29*

Girl – Iris – Eye
Eye – Needle – Pin
Pin – Firing – Range
Range – Mountain – Eyrie
Eyrie – Eagle – Griffin
Griffin – Hippogriff – Horse
Horse – Stirrup – Foot
Foot – Metatarsus – Bone
Bone – Metacarpus – Hand
Hand – Maiden – Girl

## 103. Amicable Numbers

*page 12*

220 – 284.

## 104. Alphabet

*page 49*

1. Gallop
2. Maple
3. Jays
4. Bound
5. Fizz
6. Avow
7. Quote
8. Hexes
9. Rock

## 105. Odd and Even

*page 55*

Triennially: tinily/renal.

## 106. Missing Letters

*page 33*

VS, JR. The first and last letters of the planets in orbit round the sun.

```
D I S A B L E S     B O A R D E R S
E N T R E E B Y     E P I C E N E P
C L U S T E R S     D E D U C E S A
L E D O T R O T     E R E S L E E T
A T I N E S W E     V A S S A L T T
R T O O R E A M     I T O E R A C E
E A T D E E P S     L I N D E N O R
S W A D D L E S     S C U D D E D S
```

| | |
|---|---|
| 1. Cast | 6. Wood |
| 2. Bird | 7. Body |
| 3. Land | 8. Cast |
| 4. Ball | 9. Main |
| 5. Jack | 10. Suit |

(a) rehearse, practise
(b) mitigate, increase.

| | |
|---|---|
| Benumb | Pepsin |
| Caucus | Raglan |
| Damask | Secund |
| Hyphen | Thesis |
| Kewpie | Valour |
| Larrup | Yttria |
| Nuncio | Zaffre |
| Octavo | Wallah |

## 116. Clueless Crossword

*page 31*

## 117. Crossword

*page 18*

## 118. Mnemonics

1. Initial letters give colours of the spectrum: red, orange, yellow, green, blue, indigo, violet.
2. Initial letters give planets in order from the sun: Mercury, Venus, Earth, Mars, Jupiter, Saturn, Uranus, Neptune, Pluto.
3. Initial letters give the ruling houses of England: Norman, Plantagenet, Lancaster, York, Tudor, Stuart, Hanover, Windsor.
4. The number of letters in each word coincides with pi to twenty decimal places: 3.14159265358979323846.

## 119. Not Another Pi Puzzle!

$3 + 1 \times 4 - 1 \div 5 + 9 \div 2 = 6$

## 120. The Ultimate Counterfeit Coin Puzzle

*Step A* Weigh 1, 2, 3, 4 against 5, 6, 7, 8.

*Step B* Weigh 9, 10, 11, 4 against 1, 2, 3, 8.

*Step C* There are five possibilities.

(i) If the scales were balanced both times, 12 is the counterfeit. Weigh it against another to see if it is heavy or light.

(ii) If the scales were balanced for step A but not for step B, weigh 9 against 10 to see which tips the same way as in step B. If they balance, 11 is the counterfeit (heavy or light as shown in step B).

(iii) If the scales were balanced for step B but not step A, weigh 5 against 6 to see which tips the same way as in step A. If they balance, 7 is the counterfeit (heavy or light as shown in step A).

(iv) If the scales were off-balance the same way both times, weigh 4 against another coin. If they balance, the counterfeit is 8 (heavy or light as shown in steps A and B).

(v) If the scales were off-balance in opposite ways in step A and B, weigh 1 against 2 to see which tips as 1, 2, 3 tipped in step B. If they balance, 3 is the counterfeit (heavy or light as shown in step B).

## 121. Square Words
*page 88*

(a) Eradicate
(b) Apologize
(c) Devilment
(d) Liquidate
(e) Recognize.

## 122. Odd One Out
*page 76*

A. Grove: the others are colours with the first letter missing.
B. Wheat: the others start and finish with a point of the compass.

## 123. Wot! No Vowels
*page 89*

Gypsy, myth, sylph, rhythm, tryst.

## 124. Addenda
*page 10*

| | | |
|---|---|---|
| Addenda | Deny | End |
| Adenine | Din | Ended |
| Adenoid | Dine | Indeed |
| And | Don | Iodine |
| Anode | Done | Naiad |
| Anodyne | Donee | Need |
| Dan | Donna | Nod |
| Dandy | Donnee | Noddy |
| Dane | Dudeen | Node |
| Deaden | Duenna | Nude |
| Dean | Dun | Undo |
| Den | Dune | Undine |
| Dene | Dyne | |
| Denude | Dynode | |

## 125. Monkey Puzzle
*page 92*

It rises one metre.

## 126. Steps

*page 45*

Penny – Piece
Piece – Meal
Meal – Time
Time – Step
Step – Son
Son – Net
Net – Her
Her – Ring
Ring – Worm
Worm – Screw
Screw – Ball
Ball – Cock
Cock – Pit
Pit – Bath
Bath – Bun

## 127. Letter Omission

*page 104*

1. Loathe/loath
2. Reign/rein
3. Ordinance/ordnance
4. Clothes/cloths
5. Hallow/allow
6. Appeal/appal
7. Palter/alter
8. Gait/ait
9. Yawn/awn
10. Found/fund

## 128. Eat and Drink

*page 94*

(a) F(RUM)P
(b) PY(JAM)AS
(c) B(EGG)ED
(d) (BUN)DLE
(e) (PIE)TY
(f) EN(GIN)E
(g) S(PEA)K/S(TEA)K
(h) S(HAM)E
(i) (STEW)ARD
(j) (PEAR)L
(k) GR(APPLE)
(l) S(TART)LE

## 129. Nursery Rhyme Crossword

*page 105*

## 130. Categorize

*page 94*

Anvil/drum/cochlea – connected with the ear.
Chord/arc/secant – words describing lines connected with circles.
Clef/key/scale – connected with music.
Forge/horse/shoe – connected with blacksmith.

## 131. Run Around

*page 50*

Twice.

## 132. I-frame

*page 100*

| Across | Down |
|--------|------|
| 1. Idyllist | 1. Lighting |
| 2. Impi | 2. Idly |
| 3. Implicit | 3. Innings |
| 4. Iris | 4. Illicit |
| 5. Inviting | 5. Kiwi |
| 6. Digit | 6. Instinct |
| 7. Impishly | 7. Minim |
| 8. Rigid | 8. Civic |

### 133. Fraction
*page* 12

$$\frac{5832}{17496}$$

### 134. Cheque
*page* 34

| | | |
|---:|---|---|
| £36.56 | Original |
| 56.36 | Reversed |
| 19.80 | Profit |
| − 1.52 | Spent |
| 18.28 | Remaining |

### 135. Odd One Out
*page* 42

E – the others are all 'rotated symmetric' – that is, they appear the same when turned upside down.

### 136. Grandsons Galore
*page* 44

Sixty-four.

### 137. Integers
*page* 22

Group C, obviously. But did you get Group A?

$$4 = -2^2$$
$$8 = 2^3$$

### 138. Head to Head
*page* 34

Ant 5 forwards; 4 over 5; 3 forwards; 5 over 3; 6 over 4; 7 forwards; 4 over 7, then 8 and out; 3 over 6, then 7, then 8 and out; 2 over 5, then 6, then 7, then 8 and out; 1 forwards, then over 5, then 6, then 7, then 8 and out.

# 139. Square Numbers
page 52

**Across**

| | 5 | | 1 | 8 | | | 4 |
|---|---|---|---|---|---|---|---|
| 8 | | 4 | | 6 | 4 | | |
| | 1 | | | 0 | 2 | 4 | |
| 1 | 1 | | 5 | | | | 6 |
| | | 5 | | | 9 | 2 | 9 |
| 1 | | | 9 | 3 | | 6 | |
| 9 | | 6 | | | 0 | | 4 |
| | 2 | 3 | 0 | | | 4 | |

**Down**

| 3 | | 2 | | | 7 | 3 | |
|---|---|---|---|---|---|---|---|
| | 8 | | 8 | | | 3 | 8 |
| 4 | | 1 | 6 | | | | 1 |
| | | 1 | | 2 | 9 | 6 | |
| 8 | 8 | | 4 | 9 | | | |
| | 3 | 6 | | | 2 | | 0 |
| | 6 | | 9 | 1 | | 4 | |
| 1 | | | | 6 | 1 | | 0 |

# 140. Dictionary
page 10

Queueing.

# 141. Fibonacci
page 25

No triangle can be formed with sides which equal Fibonacci numbers (5—8—13, for example, would produce a straight line, not a triangle).

# 142. Homonyms
page 79

1. Chile (chilli)
2. Beirut (bay route)
3. Stirling (sterling)
4. Laos (louse)
5. Madeira (mad era)
6. Rome (roam)
7. Bombay (bomb bay)
8. Wales (whales)
9. Amman (a man)
10. Greece (grease)
11. Taiwan (tie one)
12. Romania (rue mania)

### 143. Cross-alphabet

*page 65*

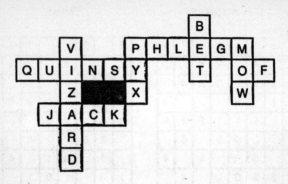

### 144. Dances

*page 43*

Hornpipe, barn, polonaise, twist, tap, folk, polka, quickstep, ballet, square, tango, reel, jig, rumba, waltz, mazurka, minuet. gavotte, jive.

### 145. All Change

*page 98*

C.

### 146. Pyramid

*page 51*

I, it, tie, tire, remit, métier, emitter, remitted, permitted.

Some variations are possible.

### 147. Palindrome

*page 16*

Detartrated.

## 148. Something in Common

*page 67*

They are all palindromes.

| | |
|---|---|
| 1. Minim | 6. Rotor |
| 2. Sagas | 7. Kayak |
| 3. Redder | 8. Level |
| 4. Shahs | 9. Civic |
| 5. Rotator | 10. Radar |

## 149. Progression

*page 81*

(a) Onerous
(b) Two-faced
(c) Three-piece
(d) Fourchette
(e) Fives
(f) Six-shooter.

## 150. Squares

*page 53*

A, D, G, H, F, B, E, C.

## 151. Magic Squares

*page 40*

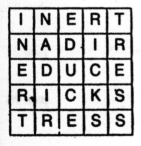
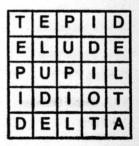

## 152. Pyramid

*page 95*

Professionalism.

## 153. Reverse

*page 51*

Spoonfed.

## 154. Collective Nouns

*page 74*

| | |
|---|---|
| Draught | of Butlers |
| Badelyng | of Ducks |
| Doppin | of Sheldrake |
| Business | of Flies |
| Murmuration | of Starlings |
| Cluster | of Spiders |
| Rafter | of Turkeys |
| Labour | of Moles |
| Bevy | of Otters |
| Down | of Sheep |
| Sounder | of Boars |
| Erst | of Bees |

## 155. Bridges

*page 48*

No, it's impossible.

## 156. Synonyme

*page 21*

*Oui/Aye.*

## 157. Small Persons

*page 75*

| | |
|---|---|
| 1. Midget | 7. Shrimp |
| 2. Pygmy | 8. Runt |
| 3. Lilliputian | 9. Homunculus |
| 4. Pipsqueak | 10. Dwarf |
| 5. Manikin | 11. Atomy |
| 6. Chit | 12. Tich |

### 158. Letter Change
*page 59*

(a) Stationary/stationery
(b) Ingenious/ingenuous
(c) Faster/Easter
(d) Allusion/illusion
(e) Coarse/course
(f) Conduit/conduct
(g) Adept/adopt
(h) Faint/feint
(i) Immanent/imminent
(j) Currant/current

### 159. Carriages
*page 37*

1. Carousel
2. Landau
3. Droshky
4. Brougham
5. Berlin
6. Barouche
7. Surrey
8. Cabriole
9. Buggy
10. Shandrydan

### 160. Division
*page 62*

$75249 \div 8361$ and $58239 \div 6471$.

### 161. Found in a Church
*page 69*

1. Nave
2. Cella
3. Aisle
4. Apse
5. Ambulatory
6. Transept
7. Chancel
8. Sanctuary
9. Hagioscope
10. Misericord
11. Pulpit
12. Ambo

### 162. Scrabble
*page 17*

| Axiom | = | 44 |
|-------|---|----|
| Thyme | = | 13 |
| Equip | = | 78 |
| Joker | = | 16 |
| Zygal | = | 76 |
|       |   | —— |
|       |   | 227 |

## 163. Collective Nouns

| | |
|---|---|
| Colony | of Frogs |
| Horde | of Gnats |
| Den | of Snakes |
| Clutter | of Spiders |
| Nest | of Machine Guns |
| Park | of Artillery |
| Doylt | of Swine |
| Gang | of Elks |
| Business | of Ferrets |
| Volery | of Birds |
| Hover | of Crows |
| Drift | of Wild Pigs |

# THE MENSA PUZZLE BOOK
## Volume 2

*Philip Carter & Ken Russell*

This second collection of Mensa puzzles presents another
dazzling range of crosswords, word and number games,
grid and diagram puzzles designed to test – and tax –
your brainpower.

# THE
# IQ
# TEST BOOK

## *Philip Carter and Ken Russell*

Arranged in three sections, this book introduces a unique concept in IQ tests – making it accessible to *all* sections of the community.

The *Culture Free* section is comprised of diagrammatical tests. They require no special knowledge of English names or words, thereby surmounting all cultural and linguistic barriers.

The *Industrial* section is a test of technical and scientific knowledge, while the *Verbal* section consists of word classifications, antonyms, synonyms and alternative meanings. Both these sections are designed to test knowledge as well as powers of reasoning and intuition.

| | | | |
|---|---|---|---|
| ☐ | The Mensa Puzzle Book 2 | Ken Russell & Philip Carter | £4.99 |
| ☐ | The Junior Mensa Puzzle Book | Ken Russell & Philip Carter | £2.99 |
| ☐ | The Mensa General Knowledge Quiz Book Vol. 1 | Ken Russell & Philip Carter | £4.99 |
| ☐ | The Mensa General Knowledge Quiz Book Vol. 2 | Ken Russell & Philip Carter | £4.99 |
| ☐ | The IQ Test Book | Ken Russell & Philip Carter | £4.50 |

Warner Books now offers an exciting range of quality titles by both established and new authors which can be ordered from the following address:

Little, Brown and Company (UK),
P.O. Box 11,
Falmouth,
Cornwall TR10 9EN.

Alternatively you may fax your order to the above address.
Fax No. 0326 376423.

Payments can be made as follows: cheque, postal order (payable to Little, Brown and Company) or by credit cards, Visa/Access. Do not send cash or currency. UK customers and B.F.P.O. please allow £1.00 for postage and packing for the first book, plus 50p for the second book, plus 30p for each additional book up to a maximum charge of £3.00 (7 books plus).

Overseas customers including Ireland please allow £2.00 for the first book plus £1.00 for the second book, plus 50p for each additional book.

NAME (Block Letters) .........................................................

..............................................................................................

ADDRESS ............................................................................

..............................................................................................

..............................................................................................

☐ I enclose my remittance for ............................................

☐ I wish to pay by Access/Visa Card

Number ☐☐☐☐☐☐☐☐☐☐☐☐☐☐☐☐

Card Expiry Date ☐☐☐☐